seat 1c

To,

LAYLA with compliments
and best wishes on your
film writing career.
Best, Fefe Mord.
3rd April 2025
LONDON, UK

seat 1c

A Survivor's Tale of
Hope, Resilience and Renewal

ZAFAR MASUD WITH
RESEARCH AND EDITORIAL INPUTS BY
SYEDA AMNA HASSAN

RUPA

Published by
Rupa Publications India Pvt. Ltd 2025
7/16, Ansari Road, Daryaganj
New Delhi 110002

Sales centres:
Prayagraj Bengaluru Chennai
Hyderabad Jaipur Kathmandu
Kolkata Mumbai

P-ISBN: 978-93-6156-098-9
E-ISBN: 978-93-6156-832-9

First impression 2025

10 9 8 7 6 5 4 3 2 1

The moral right of the author has been asserted.

Printed in India

To my parents
Because of their goodness to people
and piousness,
I am alive today.

CONTENTS

INTRODUCTION

At the beginning of 2020, a swift and deadly virus ravaged the world. The Covid-19 pandemic forced authorities to lock down cities by mid-March, yet even by early May very little was known about this novel disease. Lingering fear of the virus was compounded by a general wariness regarding government policies that had shut down businesses and slowed economic activity to a trickle. Many argued that Pakistan was too young and too fragile to survive a crisis of this magnitude. In reality, the virus had laid bare the vulnerabilities of not only a developing country like Pakistan but also of the entire globe.

The most debilitating fear was that of the unknown. Even a country like Pakistan—one that had braved terrorism, insurgencies, economic crises and rising intolerance—was now on the brink of a new, inexplicable crisis, whose end was nowhere in sight. Fear gripped the urban centres where the virus was spreading rapidly. At the time, there was no known cure and no vaccines. Treatments were a mix of trial and error. People were isolating themselves to extreme degrees, unsure whether the virus spread through touch or was airborne.

After two excruciating months of stagnancy, on 15 May, the Pakistani government tentatively allowed domestic travel again. Airlines began to dust off the jets that had lain idle in hangars and on runways for months. A tiny sliver of optimism began to seep back into society.

Pakistan is funny that way; we are often described as a resilient nation. Much of this tenacity stems largely from an untiring, and sometimes reckless, idealism that has propelled us through wars, refugee crises, earthquakes, and more. Perhaps this idealism was born of necessity, and maybe it is misplaced, but it has sunk its roots deep into the very fabric of the nation. In the bleakest of circumstances, we tend to cling to the proverbial silver lining with everything we have got.

Even amidst all the doom and gloom, I was excited. I had reason to be. I had just completed six weeks at the helm of the Bank of Punjab (BOP) and was heading home from Lahore to Karachi for the holidays. After a long career in banking and finance, I had been hesitant to join the BOP. After all, my consultancies paid well and allowed for more flexible work schedules. But after living in Pakistan for most of my life and witnessing the struggles the fledgling state had endured, I had internalized the sense of collective responsibility that so many of my country men and women share. I knew that five years as the president and chief executive officer (CEO) of a state-owned bank would create more impact than consultancies elsewhere.

My enthusiasm for my work was not diminished by the prevailing sense of impending doom brought on by the pandemic. It is no wonder, then, that I boarded Pakistan International Airlines (PIA) Flight 8303 from the Allama Iqbal International Airport in Lahore without the slightest misgiving—completely oblivious to what was about to happen next.

But my euphoric hopes for the BOP, along with the nation's tentative hopefulness as the lockdown neared its end (just in time for the close of Ramadan and the beginning of Eid), were both rudely interrupted when our flight plunged towards a fiery end over Karachi. The crash left 98 people dead. I am one of just two survivors.

It was the kind of monumental event that redefines you. I found myself recalibrating my priorities, thinking more deeply about existential questions I had once breezed by and marvelling at the series of events that allowed me to survive. In the time that followed, I also spent a lot of time grappling with painful physical complications from my injuries, which required multiple surgeries abroad.

The process of coming to terms with my mortality and my newfound physical limitations was both isolating and incredibly humbling in equal measure. On the one hand, I was alone in my predicament—in going through a devastatingly traumatic event that very few people could claim to have experienced and survived—and on the other, I was, paradoxically, awash with an outpouring of love and support that left me reeling with gratitude and awe. I finally understood what it meant to feel alone in a crowd, and it was disorienting.

Surviving a plane crash does that to you—it introduces incongruous thoughts you never imagined could exist in your brain. You feel horrified and devastated by the tragedy surrounding you, yet simultaneously, you also feel relieved at your survival. And despite that relief, you question why you survived. And when that survivor's guilt gains so much as a toehold in your mind, you find yourself wracked by it. You recognize that what happened was senseless, but you still search for meaning in the debris left behind. It becomes a constant, unrelenting struggle—finding and coming to terms with grief and joy, pain and relief, depression and a renewed will to live—all at once.

Like most people who have not experienced a traumatic event, I had never given much thought to how these complex emotions could chase one another through a survivor's mind with such blinding rapidity. So, when I confronted these discomfiting yet revelatory thoughts, I did the only thing I could think of—write a book about it. And when I was writing it, I found myself exploring everything, from the mechanics of the crash to my feelings during recovery.

■

In this book, while I do discuss the details of the crash itself—and how the fractious politics and economic crises combined to create the roiling mess that sank the overall domestic ecosystem—in the first two chapters, this is not the primary focus. Instead, the bulk of the book takes readers through 10 lessons that I learnt during and after the crash.

In the chapter titled 'Miracles', I reflect on the unlikely events that saved my life and the guilt I felt over my survival, using it as a lens to question how we perceive miracles through centuries of cultural and religious conditioning. This conditioning led me to believe I had to be *worthy* of being saved, and I struggled to explain why I had received such a miracle. The more emotionally intelligent among us know that trying to become 'worthy' of a miracle is futile; anyone with any sense of humility realizes that that goal is unattainable. It was only when I accepted that I had been granted this miracle for no reason at all that I began to overcome my guilt.

In 'Arrogance', I discuss how systemic arrogance has led to an industry-wide collapse, and how it affects individuals and business leaders. When leaders begin to rest on their laurels, empires fall. This is largely what has happened to the domestic aviation industry as a whole, and it was reflected in the actions of the pilot and ground control crew on the fateful day of my crash.

In 'Rituals', I reveal how the ground control officers had abandoned their posts to offer prayers, as my plane was about to crash. I also delve deeper into the history of ritualistic behaviour, from hoarding during the Metal Ages to modern Muslim practices. I consider both the rigidity and sacrifice that some prescribed rituals entail, and the scientifically backed benefits of ritualistic behaviour, such as its anxiolytic effects on athletes or on fishermen sailing in storm-tossed seas. While rituals can offer great comfort, many have become divisive, political and distracting. I urge readers not to become rigid in their pursuit of ritual perfection.

In 'Dues', I follow people who have had near-death experiences (NDEs), from mountaineers and geologists of the 19th century to participants in contemporary research studies. Almost unanimously, they have experienced a blinkering of time and a sense of tranquillity, and many have been reminded of their debts to other people, whether emotional or financial. I describe the moments before the crash, before I passed out, and reflect on what I have in common with these NDEs, and how that has changed my perspective towards life.

In 'Willpower', I discuss what it is like to constantly adapt to a new normal for my body, to struggle with the cognitive dissonance between how I see myself and how well my body can function. Four years after the crash, I continue to deal with surgeries and medical complications, and am compelled to familiarize myself with new areas of medical research. Just recently, doctors discovered a spinal cord displacement that has put me back in a wheelchair for extended periods, so I must now learn about osteopathy. But even though I was not an athlete before the crash, my mind has, curiously, found light and hope in the examples of individuals who have developed extraordinary willpower, from ancient Athenians who inspired marathons to endurance athletes today.

In 'Bold Steps', I examine historical examples of boldness in the face of insurmountable odds, which have withstood the tests of time and galvanized people for centuries. I am not so vain as to compare my journey with these grandstands. For us today, boldness does not have to mean macho displays of bravery in battle. In fact, it may very well be the opposite; having the strength to reject traditional ideas of stoic suffering and refusing assistance. For me, it meant being unafraid of the stigma attached to seeking mental help in Pakistan and speaking openly about therapy, even while I was leading a major financial institution in the country.

In 'Goodness', I explore how philosophers across time and place have been obsessed with nailing down true human nature, and how our literature and popular culture tend to veer towards mankind's villainy. I argue that this is not borne out of truth, but from our attraction to what makes a more interesting story. I also look at the elitist assumption that carries through many texts that discuss how the masses can be violent and must therefore be controlled, and dismiss it in favour of John F. Freie's contention that people often come together following disasters.[1] My experience after the crash as well as the communities that have sprung up after natural disasters in Pakistan certainly bear witness to this innate goodness. Rethinking our view of the 'masses' can have ramifications for things like policy design, more humane healthcare for the terminally ill and even marketing.

In 'Sincerity', I reflect on how sincerity is often sacrificed at the altar of simplicity of narrative or for political gain. While we are quick to recognize insincerity in narratives far removed from us—such as historical accounts of colonial expansion written from the point of view of the aggressor—we are not so quick to pounce on it when it affects us directly. I discuss Pakistani society's current obsession with portraying a 'good' image in international media, contrary to ground realities. I also dismiss false narratives that portray me as a saint after my survival and encourage readers to think critically about the beliefs we hold and the lengths we are prepared to go to in order to uphold those ideals.

In 'Communication', I explore how humanity has constantly worked towards communicating its experiences, from cave paintings to modern literature, and how isolating the study of communication and literature from more 'practical' pursuits like finance and economics has made us poorer. I also discuss how communicating with my family and my employees helped me heal and build more robust relationships after the crash.

Finally, in 'Legacy', I discuss how this entire experience has shaped me and led me to rethink my approach to life and what I hope to leave behind. In the Afterword, I use my experiences to argue for a more empathetic approach to life.

▪

In writing this way, I consider this book to be part memoir, part essay. I share not just an adrenaline-fuelled personal story of loss, hope and survival against the odds, but also the lessons I have learnt about life after more than two years of emotional and physical recovery, alongside measured reflective thought.

And so I share my story earnestly; by placing the

lessons I learnt at the heart of the book, my hope is that it encourages readers to question long-held beliefs, propels them into action or helps them slow down. I hesitate to call this a self-help book. For me, it is much more than a prescription of dos and don'ts. If this book succeeds in reducing your cynicism towards the world, even a tinge, it will have achieved its objective. If you feel even slightly inclined to crack the hardened shell you may have developed to deal with the world as it stands today, I will feel fortunate to be a part of that journey.

This text is both a labour of love and a means of catharsis for me. I have come out the other side with a stronger, clearer sense of who I am and what this renewed lease of life means to me. I feel incredibly lucky to have survived, and luckier still to have gained such clarity about my goals in life and the legacy I want to leave behind. I have discovered the sincerest, utmost conviction that I want to be remembered as an agent of change. If I fail to do this on a grand, global scale, I would be happy even if I positively affect the lives of the people I encounter.

Finally, this book is also my attempt to explain the unexplainable and to formulate ideas about the world that are rooted in both historical and political contexts. However, these ideas are fuelled by the urgency of someone who has faced an NDE, which often sharpens one's perspective. It has certainly done so for me, and I hope it can do the same for those who read my story.

FLIGHT 8303

On the morning of 22 May 2020, I woke up with my usual sluggishness. I loathed rising early and would avoid it whenever possible. Initially, I had booked an 11 a.m. flight on a private airline; however, the night before the flight, I discovered that PIA—the national flag carrier—was offering a special mid-afternoon flight to cater to the Eid rush. When one of my office staff asked for my preference, I chose PIA, hoping to sleep in a little longer on my day off. Bizarrely enough, I woke up much earlier than planned and could have easily caught the earlier flight.

I am generally notorious for arriving late at airports, well beyond the limits of what would be considered 'fashionably late'. But that day, I arrived early and discovered that my new protocol officer had secured me a window seat. I usually take the aisle, because it gives me room to stretch my arms and legs, so I asked him to request a change since we still had time before take-off. I was allotted 1C, an aisle seat in the very front row.

I was in good spirits as I boarded the flight. When you fly often, travelling by air no longer feels glamorous. At most, you find ways to pass the hours and ignore the drudgery of the process. On that day, however, my general listlessness at the tedium of flying was diminished by the excitement I felt about my career, my bank and the prospect of seeing my family. While I had previously held positions that allowed me to bring what I felt were meaningful changes to the banking and finance ecosystem in Pakistan, I was certain that I would be able to do much more in my current stint as the CEO and president of the BOP.

This was not my first brush with the public sector. I had served as director general of National Savings at the Ministry of Finance for two years, and had initiated a digital transformation of the organization, introducing online banking and ATM cards with the support of the Bill & Melinda Gates Foundation, the UK government's Department for International Development (now replaced by the Foreign Commonwealth & Development Office) and the World Bank. I had also tried to make the sector more inclusive, launching welfare products for the differently-abled and the families of soldiers martyred in battle. This experience had been pivotal in cementing my belief that I could be of greater service within the public sector.

I had also been a board member of the State Bank of Pakistan, and the prestigious Monetary Policy Committee, along with other crucial public bodies like the Port Qasim Authority, which regulated one of Pakistan's largest ports.

Additionally, I served on the board of Oil & Gas Development Company Limited, and am still serving as its non-executive chairman. This is one of Pakistan's largest entities and the country's only public sector company listed on the London Stock Exchange. Most importantly, my time as director general of National Savings helped me understand and appreciate how the hardcore public sector works.

In contrast, my work with private companies like InfraZamin Pakistan and Burj Capital, the investment firm I founded for renewable power development projects and investment banking, equipped me with a head for business and entrepreneurship and helped cultivate a pragmatic approach towards reforming the public sector. I had also spent years working for private banks like Barclays and Citibank.

In some ways, then, my entire career had been a dogged marathon run leading me towards the helm of the BOP, where I could finally implement the more ambitious changes I had been itching to make for a long time. The bank was brimming with potential, and I could have a hand in turning around a state asset, which I viewed as the public's collective asset. Despite its reputation, it was well managed and the quality of its portfolio was very good. It was the perfect launching pad for some of my ideas. And so, I was admittedly very proud of where I had landed, and even the monotony of flying was not going to dampen that enthusiasm.

The flight took off from Lahore at 1305 hours on 22 May 2020.

▪

The take-off conditions were near perfect: Lahore's unforgiving summer had begun, with low humidity and the temperature hovering around a sweltering 37°C. A gentle wind blew from the west, disturbing only leaves and small twigs, and stirring the lighter detritus that the bustling metropolis produced. The haze that characterized Lahori evenings had not yet descended, and visibility stretched as far as 8 km.

In contrast, Karachi roiled hot and humid, with low visibility and a strong breeze that whistled through trees and power lines, and clawed at large branches. The weather conditions were still fit for landing, but as I reflect on this, I can't help but marvel at how nature had randomly, mercurially, created the subtlest Shakespearean pathetic fallacy that writers of fiction still struggle to emulate: the calm weather at departure mirrored the tranquillity within the plane, while Karachi's brewing storm hinted at the turbulence that awaited us.

Like me, 28-year-old Mohammad Zubair, a fellow passenger I had not yet met, also had no premonitions about the fate that awaited our flight. A mechanical engineer working on industrial projects around the country, Zubair, then aged 24, was a fairly frequent flyer as well. He still carries the selfies he took in the airport lounge in Lahore just before boarding, where he is looking directly at the camera with a lazy half-smile, displaying the effortless self-assuredness and languor that only the youth can manage.

For us passengers, the flight was like any other—a little

nap, a snack, some downloaded videos and the usual mix of excitement or boredom about the approaching destination.

▪

But unbeknownst to us, as the flight approached Karachi, the control tower there had cleared the plane for an instrument landing system (ILS) approach—a method used in low visibility or poor weather, where the aircraft relies heavily on a radio navigation system and its multiple transmissions for precise guidance to land safely.

At the pilot's discretion, the flight was permitted to pass over Makli—a vast plateau known for a gargantuan, ancient necropolis that existed between the 14th and 18th centuries—which lies just 16 nautical miles from Karachi Airport. As the plane cruised over these carved sandstone graves, air traffic control warned the crew that the aircraft was higher than the required descent profile.

The flight was at 9,780 ft, instead of the required 3,000 ft, and was cruising at 245 knots.[1] The pilot could not rely on the computer to manage the descent. To quickly lose altitude, he disengaged both autopilots and extended the speed brakes using the flight control unit. Aviation experts know what this means: these breaks increase the drag on an aircraft, allowing the pilot to control the speed during a rapid descent. This was controlled chaos; the plane was poised to hurtle towards the tarmac.

It was an approach air traffic control did not agree with.

They repeatedly advised the pilot to go around once and descend gradually, but he continued the landing approach. At 7,221 ft, still 10.5 nautical miles from the runway, the pilot lowered the landing gears. Again, air traffic control suggested a go-around, but this was disregarded.[2]

Inside the cabin, I barely perceived the speed of our descent, in the absent-minded way we acknowledge changes in things we consider inconsequential. Frequent flying had robbed me of the capacity to feel wonder at the miracle of flight, or terror at any minor irregularities. As a child, I might have lingered over how a contraption of metal and electronics weighing over 60,000 kg could zip through the air. But as an adult whose work entailed travelling often, a flight was just another step in the mundane routines that comprised life.

Ground control officials, however, were becoming increasingly alarmed as the plane hurtled towards the airport. They began to beseech the pilot to ascend again. Less than seven nautical miles from the runway, at an altitude between 4,000 and 4,500 ft, air traffic control radioed, 'PIA 8303, disregard. Turn left heading 180.'[3]

Before the plane had covered even one more nautical mile, ground control reached out again through the Karachi Approach channel to reject the pilot's request to continue the approach: 'Negative, turn left heading 180.'

The final few minutes of recovered audio illustrate how confident the pilot was of his landing approach.

Pilot: We are comfortable. We can make it… We are comfortable now, and we're out of 3,500 for 3,000, established ILS 25L.

Up until this point, ground control's instructions had been clear and concise, uninterrupted by static and repeated more than once. The pilot, however, remained unmoved.

Karachi Approach: Roger, turn left heading 180.

Pilot: But we are established on ILS 25L.

Something triggered a change of heart. At an altitude of 1,740 ft and with only five nautical miles to the runway, the pilot decided to abandon the approach or perhaps second-guessed his decision, because the crew retracted the speed brakes and the landing gear into the fuselage. What compelled him is unclear; there was no radio communication discussing the change.

This was when yet another domino fell. While officials on the ground believed the aircraft was continuing the landing approach, airport communications continued through the Karachi Approach channel instead of switching over to Aerodrome Control.[4]

By then, ground control had relented to the pilot's repeated requests and cleared the plane for landing. In the ensuing chaos, Aerodrome Control failed to notice that the plane's landing gear was no longer extended. Karachi Approach received this clearance telephonically and passed it on to the pilot.

Karachi Approach: Pakistan 8303, cleared to land 25L.

Pilot: Roger, Pakistan 8303.

▪

Pakistan's Aircraft Accident Investigation Board's (AAIB) preliminary report has a graph that shows the plane's descent, mapped against the required glide path to the airport. It is as innocuous as graphs are: neutral, mathematical, precise. It is not meant to elicit feelings of despair or anger. In fact, the report warns against it in the impersonal legalese that such reports are usually written in: 'It is inappropriate to use AAIB investigation report (or any preliminary/interim report/statement by AAIB) to assign fault or blame or determine liability since neither the investigation nor the reporting process has been undertaken for that purpose.'[5]

This does not stop most people from feeling an involuntary shudder when looking at it. The irregular altitude line, representing the aircraft's descent, plunges sharply from 10,000 ft to 1,500 ft, its gradient steepening in alarming spurts. In stark contrast, the straight elegant line that represents the required approach profile hangs far below it, gently sloping downwards.[6]

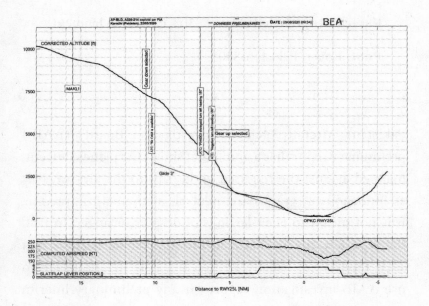

It elicits a reaction—a cold, seeping dread in the pit of your stomach that threatens to erupt—even in the mathematically challenged among us. The plane's path does not even intersect the required approach until it is just 1,500 ft above the ground. For the briefest interlude, it rises a few hundred feet again before plunging back towards the ground.

I wonder how everyone on board felt at the time. Having experienced my fair share of harried landings and bad steering, I did not give it much thought. But were there others who saw this for what it was? Did this dive nauseate someone? Was somebody else disturbed by the way their stomach lurched on the way down?

It was too early for the passengers to know what was happening or to panic. If there were any disgruntled complaints about the pilot's abilities, those murmurs were nascent, lost in the generic buzz of voices. Shattering the collective pretence of stiff politeness that humans maintain in social settings is not easy; no one wants to appear unsophisticated or naïve. And so, within the cabin, there was calm.

However, the plane's unrelenting descent was bizarre. An aircraft as sophisticated as the Airbus is equipped with multiple warning systems, and flight crews are trained to follow meticulous, and sometimes burdensome, checklists. At 500 ft, the plane was still descending at the rate of 2,000 ft per minute. It was only 15 seconds away from hitting the ground. What complicated this descent even more was the presence of illegal high-rise buildings in Model Colony, the neighbourhood adjacent to the airport. These were built in clear defiance of local laws.[7] Recordings from the flight data recorder (FDR) and the cockpit voice recorder (CVR) indicate that several alarms and alerts were going off, including overspeed warnings and ground proximity alerts. All were ignored.

When the Airbus grazed the runway during its belly landing, the engines emitted sparks as they scraped the tarmac three times, which can be seen on the CCTV footage as well, with photos taken afterwards showing the small, grey streaks they left behind. Much later, when clean-up crews scoured the area, they found debris on the runway—parts of the engine and nacelle[8] that had broken off during the first belly landing.

I realized we had aborted a landing attempt, but could not fathom how catastrophic the consequences could be. I reckoned that this was normal; planes sometimes had to change course. Zubair also felt the bumps on the ground and felt the plane ascend again. It was the familiar way one's stomach drops when planes take off or elevators go up, but like me, he was still oblivious to the peril we were in. He saw other passengers discussing what had happened, but he remained calm. To him, descending and rising again seemed troublesome, but the pilot could have done it for any number of reasons. Perhaps there was traffic on the runway.

Aerodrome Control noticed the sparks, but rather than alerting the plane directly, they relayed the information to Karachi Approach. The pilot must have felt the Airbus' frictional assault on the runway, but he never received this information from the officials on the ground.

When he discontinued the landing and decided to go around for another attempt, the landing gear was lowered for a fleeting moment and then retracted. The plane rose and began circling so that it could approach Runway 25L again. However, the engines, battered from their brush with the ground and exposed to the sparks it had produced, ignited.

Pilot: Pakistan 8303 going around.

Ground control seemed unsure of what the pilot intended, and asked for a report.

Pilot: Pakistan 8303, we would like to … come again for ILS 25L.

Karachi Approach: Roger, turn left heading 110, climb 3,000 ft.

Pilot: Left heading confirm 1…

His transmission was cut off by static, prompting Karachi Approach to ask for confirmation again.

Karachi Approach: Confirm heading 110, climb 3,000 ft.

This time, they heard the pilot.

Pilot: 110, climb 3,000 ft, Pakistan 8303.

At this point, ground control noticed that even though the pilot had confirmed the new approach, the plane was not rising to the required 3,000 ft. It was doing the opposite—*descending* long before it was meant to.

Karachi Approach: 8303, you are dropping altitude 2000 ft.

Pilot: Sir, we have … just give me 2000 ft.

Perhaps there was no time to explain why the pilot needed to fly so low. Or perhaps the crew was sticking to the pattern they had established throughout the flight—they had not followed standard call-outs. However, Karachi Approach agreed to the request.

Karachi Approach: Roger, maintain 2000'.

A few moments later, it became clear that maintaining even that altitude was a struggle. Ground control's systems showed that the plane continued downward.

Karachi Approach: Pakistan 8303, Mode Charlie showing 1,800 ft and descending.

Pilot: Copied, sir. We are now maintaining ... trying to maintain.

The pilot's tone of voice did not change. To the average listener, it appears remarkably calm on the recording. At the time, the other passengers and I were not privy to this conversation. But hearing the recording now, the shift from 'maintaining' to 'trying to maintain' sends chills down my spine. This was the pilot's first acknowledgement that things were not okay.

Ground control noticed that the plane was veering left and asked for an explanation.

Karachi Approach: Pakistan 8303, approach.

Pilot: Yes, sir.

Karachi Approach: Appear to be turning left?

Pilot: We are proceeding direct, sir. We have lost engines.

Karachi Approach: Confirm, are you going now for a belly landing?

Karachi Approach: Any runway available to land at 25.

Pilot: Roger.

The voices on the radio still exuded calm, but that was down to their training. Both the ground control officer and the pilot must have understood that the plane's best chance of survival was to make it to the runway or clear ground and crash-land on the underside of the fuselage. But the plane was still over a residential area, and on a rapid downward trajectory.

When the engines gave way, the aircraft cabin was pitted into a complete, unnerving silence while the plane was still suspended in mid-air. Zubair believes that this was when everyone began to catch on. I cannot explain how alarming complete silence is in an aircraft that is still suspended in the air, and all its engines and auxiliary power units grind to a halt.

Because I was seated in the first row, I could see the reactions of the steward seated across the aisle to my right and of the two air hostesses in front of me. When the flight crew—trained to maintain a stoic façade—begins to unravel, you know that something is wrong. The three of them had begun crying and reciting verses from the Quran.

▪

At this point, I lost consciousness. It was through others' accounts that I reconstructed what happened to me next. Zubair, however, stayed awake during the next few minutes, as the plane's power flickered on and off, and people began to crowd the walkway in their haste to reach the flight crew to ask them what was going on.

An auxiliary power unit—a small turbine that generates power from the airstream by converting wind energy into electrical energy—flickered to life. To conserve what little energy the ram air turbine was generating, the plane's computers shut down the FDR. (Later, when the authorities would sift through the wreckage, they would find no data beyond this point.) It was not enough. The plane was unable to maintain the height it needed for the belly landing. The aircrew sent out a final Mayday call:

Pilot: Sir, Mayday, Mayday, Mayday, Pakistan 8303.

His tone did not change and his voice did not rise, but the calm, measured pace of his speech was gone. He spoke furiously fast, the Maydays tripping over each other, with no room to breathe. Ground control acknowledged the report and repeated that the runways were open.

Karachi Approach: Pakistan 8303, Roger, so both runways available to land.

There was no more audio recovered after that. The hulking Airbus crashed a mile short of Runway 25L, taking down houses and cars. Zubair says the pilot was still urging people to return to their seats and keep their seat belts on when the vessel careened into a building. He is unsure what they had struck. Perhaps a water tower, he thinks. The Airbus' wings and engines caught fire, and its wreckage burst into flames on impact.

Two hours after taking off, the plane lay engulfed in flames, with the vast majority of its crew and passengers still on board—a mere 1,340 metres from the plane's intended runway at Karachi Airport. The Pakistan Civil Aviation Authority's (PCAA) preliminary report described the crash as a 'slow speed impact with high angle of attack',[9] a deduction that relied heavily on the plane's configuration and the crash site since the FDR had stopped earlier.

My survival, as one of the only two people among all lives on that plane, boggles the mind. But before I recount how I escaped, I must tell another story; a story of hubris and negligence on an organizational level that allowed this crash to happen.

1

ARROGANCE

How Hubris Turns Control into Catastrophe

My plane was just one in a long line of airline disasters. The country's flagship carrier, PIA— once a behemoth of industry and innovation—has undergone alarming institutional decay. This decline has been rapid and ruthless. In 1985, PIA had played a pivotal role in helping Emirates, now one of the world's most successful airlines, get off the ground. PIA had provided planes, technical support and trained staff for Emirates, as it had done for many fledgling airlines across the Middle East, Africa and Asia.

In 2020–21, however, despite the lockdowns and travel restrictions that followed in the wake of a global pandemic and an overall net loss, Emirates raked in US$9.7 billion in revenue, while PIA scraped the bottom of the barrel with less than $650,000.[1]

This financial performance was reflective of the general state of aviation in Pakistan over the past decade. While airlines around the world introduced luxurious long-haul flights and focused on groundbreaking innovations like sustainable aviation fuels, Pakistani airlines sank into a quagmire of fractious politics, bureaucratic processes and general decay.

Flight 8303 was the *sixth* plane to crash in Pakistani airspace within a decade. The stories of the previous five illustrate that the crash was not an isolated tragedy, but a function of systemic negligence. The AAIB's reports on these crashes provide horrifying details.[2]

▪

The first to crash was Airblue Flight 202 on 28 July 2010. Departing from Karachi, the plane crashed into the Margalla Hills near Islamabad, killing all 152 people on board.[3] At the time, the country was witnessing flash floods and torrential rains, so observers initially assumed that the freak weather conditions had caused the crash. The actual reasons, however, were far more complex.

Flight 202's captain had ignored a series of rules throughout the flight, ridiculing his first officer for his incompetence while waxing lyrical about his own prowess. Islamabad Airport is tricky to navigate even in the best of conditions, as it lies in the middle of hills and some of its runways lack an ILS. Approaching pilots have to perform a deft little manoeuvre—using the parallel runway operations to descend, and then circling around the airport to land visually at their designated runway. That day, the airport was battered by an onslaught of rain.

A landing that relies on visual confirmation must be abandoned if the runway is not visible due to reasons like bad weather. Instead of following these instructions, the captain chose to pre-programme a route that would allow the autopilot to control the descent with no input from the pilot. The point that the computer generated, to fix the plane's course and turn back towards the airport, lay well outside the recommended 8 km boundary set for Islamabad Airport. However, the captain allowed the plane to move towards it, losing sight of the airport completely. He then went below the minimum descent altitude to try to see the airport, despite warnings from ground control.

When the plane headed towards the hills, the captain stubbornly refused to listen to the alarms that were brazenly blaring across the system, or to the desperate pleas of the first officer asking to change course. As the computer warned of terrain ahead, the captain tried to turn the aircraft left, forgetting that he had placed the plane on autopilot, and wondering aloud why it refused to turn. By the time he figured out his mistake and disengaged the autopilot, he had turned the knob so far left that it had swung back to the right, and the plane veered in that direction. He then lost control of the plane, which swerved dangerously to the left and began to nosedive. After a failed attempt at pulling up, the plane crashed through the foliage and the 152 people in it (passengers and crew included) died instantly.

The last thing heard over the recording is the first officer's panicked call, which cuts off in the middle of the sentence, 'We are going down!' he screamed. 'Sir, we are going da...'

Investigators and rescue officials botched the ensuing procedures too, by wasting precious time before making attempts at recovery and being generally under-qualified (by international standards). Nobody established a security parameter, and the process of identification of bodies turned into a warped nightmare for the victims of Flight 202. In what is perhaps the shortest recorded report in aviation history, standing at 38 pages, the PCAA details what little is known about the crash.[4]

If this harrowing account sounds familiar, you are not mistaken. This interminable cycle has continued. Over and over again, qualified pilots have refused to follow standard operating procedures and ground control has missed the warning signs.

■

In November of the same year, a JetSMART Airlines aircraft, carrying employees of a foreign oil company, crashed shortly after taking off from Karachi—killing all 21 people on board.[5] One of the victims was Amer Raza, a classmate of mine from school. Though I had lost touch with Raza over the years, the news of his death was still hard to digest. Later that month, a Georgian cargo plane burst into flames and crashed at the same airport, killing 12 people.

Two years later, on 20 April 2012, Bhoja Air Flight

213 crashed in Islamabad.[6] Bhoja Airlines had suspended operations in 1999, and this was one of its first evening flights in over a decade. The plane had been purchased from a South African airline that had earlier grounded it and upgraded to a newer model. Although the PCAA officials had detected 28 faults in the aircraft during inspections, they had cleared it for flight once these were reportedly fixed.[7]

In this case, the captain and first officer were close and respected each other's boundaries. However, they were not trained to handle the aircraft's automated flight deck system in bad weather conditions. When ground control advised them that there was a gap between the storm clouds through which the aircraft could descend, the captain decided to take the opportunity. The aircraft approached the runway at 220 knots, well above the recommended 190 knots. A downward draught of air caused the plane to drop 1,000 ft in four seconds. The pilots attempted to go around instead of landing, but crashed into Hussainabad village less than a minute later. The incident claimed the lives of all 127 people on board.[8]

The fifth plane to crash during this decade was PIA Flight 661, en route from Chitral to Islamabad on 7 December 2016. Forty-seven people died, including singer-turned-religious-leader Junaid Jamshed. This time, the investigation determined that the aircraft had taken off with a fractured or dislodged turbine blade—damage that must have occurred on a previous flight. The turbine blades had crossed the recommended threshold for replacement but had not been replaced. Half an hour into the flight, evidence surfaced that suggested the left-hand propeller was no longer accurately governing speed. However, the captain and his crew failed to notice these signs.[9]

After a series of technical issues, including oil contamination and broken equipment, the crew began to lose control. The left side of the aircraft lost a 'considerable amount of drag' rapidly, and the crew overcorrected and inverted the flight, causing it to drop to almost 5,000 ft before regaining altitude, but not their composure. The drag on the left-hand side was now seven times the normal amount and the plane spiralled as if in a drunken stupor. Despite increasing inputs to the right, the pilot could not stop the aircraft from angling left whilst approaching high terrain. The plane rolled and struck the ground in a steep nosedive.

▪

Despite all these incidents of negligence or incompetence by flight crews, ground control and maintenance officials, things remained the same. Why did nothing change at the national level after five planes crashed? Why did experts continue to analyse the trajectory of the affected flights and their wreckage but fail to take concrete measures to improve passenger safety? Why did the national narrative always zero in on the mistakes of the crew but fail to question why airlines and the government exhibited such lethargy in bringing about reforms?

For years, vendors had allegedly been supplying subpar planes to Pakistan. PIA was plagued by scandals about employee hiring procedures and its failure to push for more routine plane inspections and more robust training for its flight crews. Meanwhile, the PCAA was lampooned for the lack of transparency in its investigation processes.

Corporate losses led airlines to focus on profit margins instead of flight safety, and steps were regularly skipped during upkeep, maintenance and training. The national carrier also faced embarrassment on the international front and its damage control tactics sometimes verged on the absurd. In 2016, after one of the worst air disasters of the country, PIA chose to ground its ATR-42s until an investigation cleared them for flight. Days later, as the first ATR-42 sat on the runway waiting to fly again, officials were seen dragging a black goat on to the runway in Islamabad.[10]

The goat was slaughtered on the runway to ward off the evil eye, to the amusement and chagrin of the nation. While PIA spokesmen were quick to distance themselves from the act—claiming that the ground officials had chosen to undertake the slaughter on their own—the airline became a laughing stock as headline after headline questioned the skills and abilities of its staff. It seemed as if the airline was hanging by 'on a wing and a prayer', according to one satirist.[11]

Time and again, pilots showed a blatant disregard for standard protocols and instructions, airlines and investigating agencies missed glaring issues when they cleared aircraft for flights, and crew training remained inadequate. The entire system needed to be overhauled.

■

As someone deeply entrenched in the business world, I find myself constantly thinking about this kind of large-scale institutional decay. Having held senior positions in multinational banks across Pakistan and abroad, my interest in the way that large, successful businesses, industries and even empires turn into decrepit relics of the past is not entirely triggered by the crash. It is also fuelled by the professional curiosity that keeps me going up the corporate ladder. I find examples of this decay strewn across time—in the way that national-level sports teams spiral downwards after years of seemingly perennial success, and also in the way historic empires deemed 'too large to fail' come crashing down. The single trait that precedes this downfall is almost invariably the same: arrogance.

After the crash, I was even more curious to see how systemic arrogance could lead to industry-wide collapse and affect individuals and leaders in general.

One of the first examples that springs to mind is from a foggy memory of a sport popular in Pakistan during my childhood—*thappad kabaddi*. It had once been a popular sport; my father had even dabbled in it himself while growing up in Amroha in Uttar Pradesh, India. He had been a good player. However, the sport's popularity began to wane during my childhood.

In the kabaddi pits of old Lahore and Gujranwala, known to the locals as *akhadas*, men always fought barefoot. Their bodies glistened with a thin sheen from a generous application of oil, making it easier for them to slip out of the opponent's grasp. When the whistle blew to signal the start of a match, the wrestlers began a dance of sorts—feinting punches and sidestepping fearsome blows. Eventually, one would tire of this charade and slam directly into the opponent in an effort to pummel the latter on to the ground.

These matches were fast and furious, over in a frenetic flurry of movement and stealth. The players (known as *pehelwaans* in Urdu) trained for months to win matches that would often last mere minutes. Spectators travelled from other cities to watch them train, and seats at the akhadas sold out in hours. However, when the pehelwaans began to compete on an international level, they looked down on the rules. They scoffed at the soft, synthetic material used to make the new rinks that replaced the hard, packed dirt they were used to. In order to claim a victory, they could no longer rely only on their lightning-fast reflexes. Tumbling an opponent and pinning them to the earth once was not enough; they were expected to do it again and again, building up a tally of points before the match was decided in their favour.

This variant of kabaddi became more and more convoluted. Stamina replaced speed as a player's most enviable quality, and the public began to lose interest. On the international front, the biggest names from Pakistan began to lose matches. The changing rules and the soft rings flustered them. The largest spectator sport of the 1970s was relegated to backyard akhadas and small pits.

My father used to tell me stories of men whose strength rivalled that of ancient heroes—who pulled tree trunks to train for fights and ran dozens of miles every day—who were now resigned to mediocrity. City development authorities replaced some akhadas with public buildings and cricket stadiums. Today, very few of the original akhadas remain. Those that do are home to an impoverished breed of pehelwaans, struggling with scarcity as well as the challenges of the sport.

I grew up in Lahore, a city that had once been home to some of kabaddi's greatest names, at a time when the sport's downfall had just begun. In many of its circles, the story of kabaddi's decline became a cautionary tale against the arrogance of all its stakeholders. The pehelwaans used to sneer at international competitors, mistakenly assuming that they would be able to best foreign champions merely because they had trained on 'harder' soil. They looked down on competitions that were fought on 'mattresses' instead of dirt. This self-assured cockiness destroyed any hopes of winning in international forums. As pehelwaans began to lose, the government pulled funding, perhaps believing in the invincible popularity of the sport. These were devastating overestimations that brought about the downfall of a long-beloved sport.

Gradually, prize money in local competitions went down

and pursuing a career as a kabaddi player became entirely unsustainable. Many players fell into lives of poverty and disarray, while others invested in alternative careers, often focusing on building factories or poultry farms. If only the influx of foreign players and the export of local ones had been met with a change in technique, a willingness to train flexibly and a desire to learn the new-fangled rules of the international game, kabaddi may have retained its former glory in Pakistan. Instead, the pehelwaans and trainers arrogantly clung to the old ways, loudly proclaiming how their version of kabaddi was better than the international one, even as the world around them crumbled.

Lamentably, kabaddi was not the only sport that suffered a downfall on account of the haughty inability to adapt. Pakistan's hockey teams—which won gold and silver at the Olympics during the 1960s, 1970s and 1980s—are now barely afloat. Funnily enough, hockey's downfall in the country also coincided with the game's switch to an artificial ground; as the rest of the world switched to Astroturf instead of grass fields, Pakistan's dribble and dodge tactics (painstakingly perfected on the older grounds) lost their competitive edge. This was further exacerbated by the Pakistan Hockey Federation's lack of funding and its inefficient use of what little funds did exist. Today, Pakistani hockey has fallen so far from grace that teams barely qualify for international tournaments.

It is hard to fathom how often success stories, like those of PIA or the nation's former kabaddi and hockey champions, have turned sour, given the number of cautionary stories about arrogance that litter literature and history. It is almost as if in the staid rooms, where business decisions are made and investors plot growth curves, we have forgotten the stories and legends we grew up hearing from our elders.

Perhaps it seems painfully obvious to parallel the myth of Icarus when dissecting the story of a plane crash involving arrogance, but it is also fitting. Icarus was the son of Daedalus, a genius inventor who fashioned a labyrinth on a Cretan island for his king—a maze so complex that it was essentially a prison. When Daedalus had a disagreement with the monarch who had commissioned the project, both he and his son were thrown into the labyrinth.

Daedalus knew that they would not survive on the island and desperately searched for a way out. Navigating the maze was impossible—he himself had made sure of that. Eventually, inspiration struck. They could escape the vast and dangerous labyrinth by flying out, using wings fashioned out of wax and feathers shed by beasts. Strapping Icarus into a harness, Daedalus gave him one piece of advice, the gist of which was: 'Fly too low and you will fall into the ocean. Fly too high and the sun will melt the wax holding your wings together, and you will tumble to your death.'

Icarus promised his father he would be careful, but as the euphoria of flying enraptured him, he began soaring higher and higher. Soon, Daedalus could no longer see his son. He scanned the horizon, but to no avail. Finally, he began to look towards the sea, where he saw a mass of feathers floating on the surface. The wax on Icarus' wings had melted, and he had drowned.

The tale was used in Greek literature to warn against the dangers of arrogance and overestimating one's abilities. Its message is so central to the human struggle that it has persisted across time and become popular in retellings of various forms. First-century frescoes from the ancient city of Pompeii depict Daedalus and Icarus flying out of the labyrinth. Sixteenth-century black-and-white prints show a terrified Icarus plummeting to his death. A highly stylized 1819 painting by Merry-Joseph Blondel captures the unravelling of Icarus' wings just before his fall. The myth of Icarus has even found its way into modern TV series, and has been referenced in different episodes of *CSI: NY*, *Fringe* and *Law and Order: Criminal Intent.*

These cautionary stories are popular not only because they are exciting but also because of the lessons they contain: throughout history, it has been observed a sheer number of times how humans have struggled to contain their arrogance and have suffered for it.

There was a French emperor, Napoleon I, who famously overreached and sent his entire army to be demolished by the Russians (and their allies) in the middle of an unforgiving winter. His obsession with aristocracy, coupled with his own humble origins, had propelled him into a lifetime of aggressive campaigns against neighbouring countries, in an effort to raise his own station. By 1812, he had conquered Germany, Italy, Spain and Poland, maintaining an extensive military presence in all these territories and appointing his siblings to positions of power. While his arrogance was understandable, if not justifiable, historians still struggle to understand why he refused to reach a compromise with the Russian Tsar, Alexander I.

Napoleon arrogantly believed his army could maintain the same steady pace through Russia as it had in other regions, despite facing a different terrain, brutal winters and a lack of supplies. The Tsar's army simply retreated into Russia instead of engaging directly, leaving the French troops struggling against the bitter cold and dwindling resources. In the one battle that Napoleon's army finally waged, broken in spirit and energy, he lost 70,000 men. Of the 500,000 soldiers who had set out with him, only 200,000 survived. French nobles spent very little time in deposing him at home. While the disgraced emperor spent some energy trying to regain what he had lost, he spent his remaining days in exile.

Closer to home, there were the cocky Mughal rulers who failed to consolidate power at the centre of their sprawling empire, only for a British trading company to wrest control away from them. When the East India Company (EIC) first came to undivided India in the 17th century, they had just been ousted from Southeast Asia's spice markets by the Dutch. The EIC's initial foray into the Mughal court was as supplicants asking for trading rights. The Mughals, presiding over a vast empire and riches, saw no threat from a mere merchant organization. Emperor Jahangir allowed them to build bases on the Indian coasts. Having established a firm toehold on the Indian subcontinent, the EIC began to travel inward, trading spices and textiles while testing the waters for rebellion.

Meanwhile, the peripheral areas of the Mughal empire were so spread out that they barely had control. They ran on a system of *mansabdari*, whereby local leaders raised armies and fought for the Mughals if the need arose. This system made them only slightly more loyal than mercenaries; money drove loyalty. When the Mughal coffers began to dry up a couple of centuries later, some of these armies began to lose interest in defending the throne. According to historians Ayesha Jalal and Sugata Bose:

> The weakening of the Mughal emperor and nobility [in the centre] enabled the strengthening of other groups [...] Hindu and Muslim revenue farmers, mainly Hindu and Jain merchants and bankers, and mostly Muslim service gentry. The merchants and bankers in particular provided critical financial sustenance to the regional states of the eighteenth century. This paved the way for a process of commercialization of political power and social relations.[12]

In some of the far-flung states, independent kingdoms began consolidating what the Mughals had kept separate; this allowed these kingdoms to slowly gain control of the financial and political systems. States like Bengal and Awadh began to shift away from the merit-based appointments followed under the mansabdari system to patriarchal holdings, and started relying on merchant bankers like the Jagat Seths of Bengal.[13]

The Sikhs, Jats and Marathas began to rally for independence from the Mughals, and other local kingdoms, such as the Rohilla sultanates and small kingdoms in Deccan India, began to clamour for more autonomy. With increasing financial sovereignty through trade, these states did not even need to rely on the merchant bankers to sustain themselves in the absence of Mughal support.[14] However, in states where merchant bankers were active, the balance of power shifted towards them significantly and they began to control most of the finances and political power.[15] In some instances, they even had powers of the state where they operated.

Recognizing the commercial opportunities, these bankers began to offer support to the EIC. All of this paved the way for British takeover. But the Mughals—far too comfortable in the luxury and flattery afforded to them by their central states—took little notice of what was happening in the outer reaches of their empire. The EIC slowly expanded its influence and began to take over states, first through financial means and later through political and military scheming. By 1818, the EIC controlled over two-thirds of the Mughal Empire.[16]

While reports of the Mughals usurping local resources are exaggerated (riots against them occurred in some of the richest provinces), successive Mughal emperors were so sure of their power and so dismissive of local concerns that they made this transfer of power easier for the EIC.

In fact, colonial expansion has been uncannily congruent across the globe. In Africa—where I was posted for two and a half years as the regional managing director and CEO of Barclays for Zambia, Botswana and Zimbabwe—I encountered historical accounts that were hauntingly familiar. In the stories I heard from friends and colleagues, I was reminded of the vehemence and arrogance of the colonial engine tearing through the world. The European colonizers had exacerbated local tribal differences in Africa too, in an attempt to divide and rule, and a similar pattern had emerged. The only difference in strategy was the degree of brutality. While the Indian subcontinent was largely subjected to financial, political and military means, the African people were subjected to the inhumane slave trade.

Much like the British in India, European powers in Africa coerced African chiefs to collaborate with them by first using 'material inducements';[17] they encouraged consumer demands for European goods and bartered for slaves captured from other tribes. According to an article, 'They formed military alliances to instigate fighting and increase the number of captives, and shifted the location of disembarkation points for the trade along the West and Central African coast to follow African military conflicts.'[18]

This demonstrates a barbaric and entirely unethical exploitation of local customs, driven by arrogance and greed. In his scathing critique of the European colonial endeavour, Walter Rodney wrote that the European slave trade impoverished the Africans not only monetarily but also via social violence. It removed millions of youths—whom Rodney dubbed the 'human agents from whom inventiveness springs'[19]—from the continent, and through the expatriation of African surplus, contributed to the capitalist development of Europe while Africa remained underdeveloped. I do not lay the blame of colonization at the feet of the colonized, but I can see how replacing the local self-assured arrogance in dealing with these nefarious outsiders with a more wary approach could not have hurt.

If you grow up in Pakistan, you are introduced to many of these stories, in which a pervasive sense of arrogance brings about the downfall of mythic heroes, sports teams and even sprawling empires. In retelling these stories, arrogance is portrayed as an unforgivable sin, and yet it pervades our society and organizations.

▪

Perhaps it is unfair to assume that the plane I was on crashed solely due to arrogance. After all, then, only information I have is from a preliminary report of the incident. Yet, I keep returning to the flight crew's insistence on attempting to land a plane that was still at a high altitude. In fact, standard operating procedures had been ignored ever since the flight took off. The crew did not make the required callouts before undertaking changes in the flight plan and ignored crew resource management guidelines throughout the flight. Meanwhile, the control towers failed to communicate critical information to the aircraft crew, and for an aircraft that had remained grounded for 46 days during quarantine, a detailed analysis of maintenance records was, and is still, not available.

And then there were the obvious issues I mentioned earlier. Had the pilot not displayed such blatant disregard for the advice from ground control and, apparently, from his first officer, the plane might have landed on its initial descent. The engines would not have grazed the ground and later burst into flames. I believe it was the arrogance of the pilot that led to the crash.

Moreover, my flight fell on the last Friday of Ramadan, a day that holds special significance in Muslim tradition. The vast majority of the crew on the ground had wanted to make use of this once-a-year occurrence to offer their Friday prayers, leaving the control room understaffed. While I understand the religious fervour that led them to leave their posts, I cannot fathom why the standard operating procedures simply did not account for such an event (given that the staff was overwhelmingly Muslim) and encourage the crew to offer their prayers in shifts.

The individual mistakes of the flight and ground crew are not the biggest problem Pakistan has with aviation today. Perhaps there were parameters we do not understand, alongside circumstances that compelled the crew to act as they did—fuelled by a situation that would vault most functional adults into a state of heightened panic or emotional paralysis. What is unforgivable though is the fact that this arrogance seems to be systemic and pervasive.

PIA, once a respectable airline, is now an organization that reeks of stagnancy, nepotism and corruption.

In June 2020, a month after my plane crashed, PIA grounded 150 of its 434 pilots over claims that their licences were invalid.[20] Although it was later revealed that these claims were unfounded, the damage to the airline and the country was already done. Passengers were told that some flights would be cancelled. The International Air Transport Association (IATA) called this a serious lapse in safety protocols,[21] while international aviation experts expressed their shock yet again. The embarrassment did not end there. Six months later, in January 2021, a PIA aircraft was seized in Malaysia following a court order, as part of a US$14 million lease dispute.[22] Passengers were given an alternative ride home, although PIA officials were livid, calling the treatment unacceptable.

However, as the records from the past decade indicate, PIA is far from the only problem we have. The state airline has at least begun a drive to acquire newer planes and sell off older acquisitions that should now be grounded. When its finances took a hit because of the pandemic, the airline also shed excess weight by returning leased aircraft to foreign firms and cutting its workforce by 2,000 employees.

The problems identified earlier are not limited to PIA; they pervade the entire aviation industry in Pakistan. If Pakistan's domestic flight standards cannot be brought in line with international ones, and if standardized procedures to handle crashes and their aftermath cannot be enforced, then these crashes should not be treated as isolated tragedies; they should be recognized for what they are—casualties of a system that continues to flout safety requirements, either because it is cheaper to do so or because its organizational culture prizes displays of confidence over passenger safety.

Either way, the aviation industry in Pakistan would benefit from an injection of humility, an eagerness to consider the mistakes of the past and a focus on passenger and crew safety. It is an industry rife with overconfidence and mass delusion. A more rigorous investigation into its protocols and procedures may help address these issues.

As a victim of an organization that has fallen from grace for exactly the above reasons, I hope that we can begin to take leadership training seriously, even in times of crisis. If you find yourself in a position of power, surround yourself with people who are smarter than you, ask questions, open yourself up to feedback and rub shoulders with the most junior staff you have hired. You will find your perspective and level of humility greatly altered.

I still believe that the crash that claimed 97 lives and completely upended another two was entirely avoidable. If the pilot had not displayed such hubris in ignoring the advice that multiple skilled officials had sent him with mounting urgency, the plane may have landed safely. The idea that his judgement of the situation could outweigh the rigorously developed protocols for landing, or that the opinions of the staff members who were clearly lower in the hierarchy could be summarily dismissed, is ridiculous. The fact that this attitude was accepted in an organization that routinely loses its planes in high-casualty accidents is even more confounding. Yet, it has happened time and again. Unless our airlines completely overhaul their organizational cultures and rethink their approach to management, it will continue.

▪

Even on an individual level, arrogance serves no purpose. At best, it lowers others' opinion of you; at worst, your inflated sense of self can have disastrous consequences for those around you. I do not claim to be aggressively humble, but a decent dose of humility and self-reflection can keep disaster at bay. Not all of us are pilots in charge of hulking pieces of metal lurching through the sky, but we are all susceptible to the occasional self-congratulatory thought.

So, how energetically should we defend ourselves against such thoughts? When I ask myself this question, I am usually reminded of Rais Amrohvi's couplet (he was a celebrated scholar and poet, and my grandfather's elder brother):

Kehne lage ke humko tabahi ka gham nahin
Maine kaha wajah e tabahi yahi toh hai
Hum log hain Azaab e Ilaahi se bekhabar
Sabse bada Azaab e Ilaahi yahi toh hai

They said we are not afraid of being destroyed;
I said that is the cause of destruction.
We are all unaware of His divine punishment
And that is the biggest divine punishment of all.[23]

In his simple, unadorned poetry, Amrohvi gets to the heart of the matter: when we forget that we can be destroyed or that we are not too big or too important to fail, we bring about our own destruction.

But when a system is already rotten, how much worse can it be due to individual arrogance? A lot, it turns out. In the 1980s, psychologist James Reason sought to understand why so many road accidents occurred in the UK.[24] He conducted a survey, questioning over 500 people about their perceptions of their own driving skills. Reason asked specific questions, such as: How many violations or infringements were on their record? How many times did they check their rear-view mirror or enter the wrong lane?

Surprisingly, nearly everyone felt that they were better than the average driver, even when their presence on the road posed an active threat to everyone else sharing that space. This mass delusion or inflation of one's abilities is now known as the 'better-than-average effect'.[25] It is almost universal; people rank themselves higher than others across most parameters.

This overconfidence can lead to fatal errors, as in the case of our airline pilots in recent years, but it has repercussions in every field. It can lead to diagnostic errors in medicine, unwarranted convictions or acquittals in law, and unhappy children in education. A recent study also indicates that arrogance is contagious.[26] It is no wonder, then, that Napoleon's army charged into battle without a hope of winning, or that our Mughals gave away large tracts of land to foreigners without tightening central control.

In our personal lives, we should be equally vigilant against making lazy, inflated assumptions about our abilities. If you find yourself subconsciously slipping into this habit, make a conscious and concerted effort to remedy it. Remember that advocating for your ideas in any situation, personal or professional, should not come at the cost of overshadowing other points of view. Give others the space to safely and openly express their ideas, without trivializing their input, and try to understand their perspectives.

This may be one of the best ways to keep yourself from developing an unwarranted sense of self-importance. Focus on listening and invite different opinions on everything. Never assume that your religious, political or professional beliefs are beyond discussion because of their inherent superiority. When you are met with views that are different from your own, assume that they may have value and engage with them instead of being dismissive. This does not mean that you must give equal weight to good and bad ideas, but that you must take the time to consider each idea's worth before making decisions. Never assume your ideas are above criticism or debate.

I have made this mistake myself. When I was working at Barclays in the southern Africa region, a new wave of global management came in and began to make hasty changes to the top leadership. Instead of waiting to see what they would do or engaging with them, I decided to leave the bank and take on another opportunity that had presented itself. Barclays had done very well under my leadership, and the idea of defending myself and my ideas to prove my worth rankled. Had I stayed, I might have continued a long and lucrative career with the bank, but I isolated myself instead. The trajectory of my career afterwards leaves me with little justification for regretting this choice, but my reaction to the issue could have been better.

This is why even when you are making objectively correct decisions, feedback is important. If you have any kind of hierarchical power, whether as the head of a department or the head of a household, or even as the eldest sibling, acknowledge that you are susceptible to making lazy assumptions about your ideas being right. It is imperative for you to develop the habit of actively listening to those around you.

In addition to building better relationships, fostering empathy and improving your problem-solving abilities, listening to others will help them feel valued. It is a sign of respect that we owe to those around us. And if you ever find that you have begun isolating yourself as the only person capable of making decisions that affect others, whether personal or professional, stop and question why. Actively listening to others and learning to concede when you are wrong and apologizing (a trait I learnt from my father) will naturally stave off the unhealthy egotism that we are all susceptible to developing.

2

DUES

Reflections on Obligation and
Peace in the Face of Death

Before we turn our attention to the steaming wreck that so violently interrupted the stillness of suburbia in Model Colony, I must take a brief interlude to discuss what happened when the plane's engines had just stopped working. I cannot flippantly glide by the 'existential slap'[1] that jolts your system when your mind first acknowledges that death may be close. It is too monumental a feeling to be hastily described amid descriptions of technical failure.

At the time, the flight crew had already buckled themselves into the seats opposite and beside me, and the cockpit door had flown open. I could see that the crew members were bracing themselves for the worst, and I knew with irrevocable certainty that their fears were not misplaced.

Yet, as I thought about the impending crash, a voice inside me told me that I was going to survive. I remember being completely embroiled in an argument with this voice. I must have experienced that brief ripple in the space–time continuum that survivors of NDEs have spoken about, for it felt as though I had all the time in the world to convince the voice about the logical outcome of a crash.

I told myself, 'Look, this crash is inevitable. There is no way it will be averted.' And still, I heard the same response from within me—the unshakeable belief that I would survive, even if the plane crashed. I know the more cynical among you will chalk this experience down to the ravings of a man facing death. Perhaps I was just reverting to my default setting; as a single man, I often talked with myself, so this experience was not singular.

I can say it was every bit as profound as those before me have described, if not quite as dramatic. There was an unflappable calmness—a steadiness that pervaded all my thoughts and my being. I contemplated the plane crashing and saw the panic around me, but it was not mirrored within me. It was not exactly a numbing of my thoughts; I did not feel disembodied or removed from the situation, but my thoughts were not frenzied or fearful. In fact, they had the penetrative clarity that many survivors speak about. At the time, I had not read about NDEs, so I could not place my feelings within an existing body of anecdotal data. I just knew what was about to happen and that it was going to be all right. Later, amid a long and laborious recovery, my thoughts kept returning to that moment, and I discovered the stories of other people who had experienced something similar in their NDEs, such as the story of Albert Heim.

▪

In 1871, geologist Albert Heim led an educational trip to Säntis, the crown peak of the Alpstein massif in Switzerland. He was one of the first geologists to render a model of the peak and its surroundings. While his contribution to the study of mountain formation and glaciology is formidable, that is not why his story interests me.

On that fateful afternoon in 1871, the doctoral candidate was leading a group down an icy slope on Säntis' side when he slipped and slid off a cliff, falling almost 60 ft. Heim remembered this fall vividly. In the brief moments as he slid and tumbled down the mountain, it was as though his mind disentangled itself from the paltry restrictions of time. What he felt in those five to ten seconds, he later said, could not be described in 'ten times that length of time'.[2]

In the midst of the fall, Heim made a decision: if he survived, he would muster up the strength to call out to his colleagues so they would not endanger themselves by hurrying down. He also thought about how he would not be able to give the inaugural university lecture he was scheduled to deliver five days later. Despite the flood of thoughts during those brief moments, he appeared to have had sufficient time to mull them over and a deep calm pervaded his mental state.

This distortion of time and the feeling of tranquillity fascinated Heim so much that, later in his life, when he was an established professor of geology at the University of Zurich, he would return to it with a scientist's eye. He reached out to as many mountaineers as he could with a simple question: What did mountaineers experience when they fell?

In February 1892, he presented his collection of other survivors' accounts at the Swiss Alpine Club in Zurich. A translation of his paper was later published in *OMEGA* in 1972, an academic journal dedicated to 'death and dying'. And so, what started as an accidental, transcendental experience on a chilly mountainside in the Alps became an obsession that led to the first scientific study of NDEs.

One of the mountaineers Heim briefly mentioned was Edward Whymper, whose story was one of tragedy and triumph, and whose observations about his own NDE were hauntingly similar to Heim's. Before Whymper and his companions summited the Matterhorn in 1865, no one had been able to successfully make the ascent. Of his three companions and three guides, only two guides survived the perilous trip. The seasoned mountaineer had tried to climb the notoriously unforgiving peak three times before. In 1861, during one of these previous attempts, Whymper lost his footing and fell nearly 200 ft down a steep gully, sliding to a halt near a precipice that hung 800 ft over a glacier. He had the presence of mind to use a big lump of snow as a plaster around his bleeding head before passing out, and it was not until hours later that he was able to slowly make his way down the mountain and get help. Curiously, Whymper also described a slowing of time during which he felt calm and peaceful as his mind replayed many memories. 'I was perfectly conscious of what was happening, and felt each blow; but, like a patient under chloroform, experienced no pain ...'[3]

Heim's work initiated a wave of research into NDEs, and the people studying them began to see common threads among them. Much of this research was not grounded in medicine, but in the accumulation of experiential knowledge. Nevertheless, it makes for fascinating reading. Survivors of mountaineering accidents, traffic accidents and shipwrecks often reported seeing panoramic memories,[4] leading to the popular trope of 'one's life flashing before one's eyes'.

This trope has permeated literature, art and popular media for centuries, with references to NDEs appearing in works as old as Plato's *The Republic* to Samuel Taylor Coleridge's 'The Rime of the Ancient Mariner'. What is curious, though, is that literary or artistic representations of NDEs are not always positive. Nowhere is this more evident than in *127 Hours*—Danny Boyle's gripping movie about a man whose arm gets stuck under a boulder in a canyon. In one of cinema's most fear-inducing moments, Boyle's protagonist (based on Aron Ralston) saws off his own arm to escape. Boyle's version of an NDE is one that is stretched out over five days, so there is no sense of calm, only an excruciating, hellish realization of one's own mortality.

Depictions like these might be why humankind has a collective fear of death. I am not claiming they are inaccurate, but they are in sharp contrast to most collected reports of NDEs, which seem to be surprisingly peaceful. In 1980, Kenneth Ring's collection of anecdotal reports of NDEs suggested that 60 per cent of subjects felt peace.[5] The following year, cardiologist Michael Sabom reported that such feelings existed in all of his subjects.[6] Bruce Greyson—who analysed over 1,500 reports of NDEs in patients admitted to a cardiac inpatient service—claimed that 85 per cent felt peace and 67 per cent felt joy.[7] Olaf Blanke, Nathan Faivre and Sebastian Dieguez, who compiled these numbers in their study of out-of-body and NDEs, wrote:

> Many subjects also report feelings of absolute love, all-encompassing acceptation, often by a supreme entity which is associated with a radiant light. Nevertheless, NDEs may also be associated with negative emotions, 'hell'-like features, encounters with tormentors or frightfully devoid of any meaning. The exact incidence of such negative NDEs is not known, but is assumed to be rather low.[8]

All of this anecdotal data seems to suggest that people who survive impossible situations feel something profound and contracted, and many have resulting shifts in attitudes and behaviour. But we do not yet understand *why* these experiences occur. In addition to the life review, people have also reported seeing ghostly apparitions (often of deceased family members), experiencing a sense of oneness with the world, a narrowing of vision (which often manifests as a light at the end of a tunnel) or a sense of disembodiment (the eerie feeling that one is hovering just above one's body, another image that pervades horror movies and TV).

▪

I, for one, am not content with relegating experiences so profound to chemical imbalances in the brain or the misfiring of neurons brought on by stress. What drew me to survivors' accounts were both the similarities and differences that this multitude contained.

One thing that leapt out at me, in addition to all the commonalities identified by researchers before me, was how obligations seemed to fight their way to the forefront of the survivor's mind—even when they were wrestling with much more consequential thoughts. Heim had been concerned about a lecture he had promised to give. A century and a half later, another plane crash survivor, Ric Elias, spoke about how his last thoughts were of his wife and family, and his will to eliminate negative energy from his life.[9]

It is telling of the human condition that so many survivors—separated by decades and experiences—all recalled their obligations to other people, whether trivial or weighty. This was more indicative of my experience than the rosy clouds and orchestral music that some have described.

While the time between my plane's engine catching fire and the eventual crash must have spanned a few minutes, I only recall a crucial 30 seconds or so. In those 30 seconds I knew without a shadow of a doubt that my plane was going to crash. The engines had lost power. By Zubair's account, this happened more than once, but I was only conscious for that first time.

Even as I experienced the moment of clarity and deep introspection I described earlier, I do remember thinking about a somewhat trivial obligation, much like Heim. As clichéd as it sounds, my entire life flashed before my eyes, as if a truly prodigious artist had laid it all out on a canvas with brilliant strokes. I did not have any significant regrets, but there were things I wished I had done earlier. I was reminded of Munir Niazi's poem, 'Hamesha der kar deta hun', a tragicomic ode to procrastination:

> *Hamesha der kar deta hun main har kaam karne*
> *mein*
> *zaruri baat kehni ho koi vaada nibhana ho*
> *usse awaaz deni ho usse vapas bulana ho*
> *hamesha der kar deta hun main*[10]

Our English translation does not quite do justice to the simplicity of form and language with which Niazi laments the delays in his life, but it gives an idea of the sentiment:

> I always leave things too late
> If I ever have something important to say or a
> promise to keep
> If I need to reach out to her or call her back
> I always leave things too late

During those final moments on that plane, I did not believe I had ever done anything that I needed to apologize for or anything that would cause anguish. But I did dwell on the smaller things: perhaps I had not shown enough affection to the most important people in my life, and now I had run out of the opportunities to do so. I also thought of more practical matters; I wished I had signed my life insurance papers instead of procrastinating, so my mother could receive a substantial amount as my only beneficiary in the event of my death. Maybe that was the banker in me, pragmatic to the end. Soon after that, I fainted.

▪

I am not an overtly religious or superstitious man. I always thought I would set my score based on scientific knowledge more than anything else. But what I experienced during those moments of lucid thought has left a lasting impression on me. It does not matter whether the calm conversation I had with myself can be explained by neurological synapses firing in a unique pattern owing to stress, or whether I experienced a more transcendental, spiritual state that took away pain and fear. What matters is my experience of it, and the obligation I had to my mother and to my siblings.

As the oldest sibling, and the one solidly cemented in finance, I had the responsibility of managing my parents' inheritance. I was the only one with knowledge of their financial affairs, and my death would have left my siblings without a clue about how to handle everything. My parents had probably thought, as most parents do, that I would outlive them. To make things easier for all their children, they had placed a lot of property in my name—since I had already taken on the mantle of a fatherly figure for my younger siblings. I shudder to think about the financial quagmire I would have left behind if I had died. So now, more than ever, I believe in clearing my debts. As soon as I began recovering from my trauma, I started clearing all dues.

I came to realize that our ideas about relationships stemming from filiation are decidedly one-sided. Even though Eastern or Asian societies do not tout individualism as a virtue to the degree that Western ones do, many of us subconsciously believe it was our parents' obligation to raise us well (since they chose to have us), while our obligations in return are somewhat more limited. This kind of thinking reduces relationships to a calculation—a mathematical equation we are constantly trying to balance with military precision. When I say we 'owe' our parents and loved ones, it is not to foster this kind of transactional thinking. Healthy, loving relationships cannot be formed on the basis of what you believe you owe in response to what you have been given. Rather, they are built on the basis of what you *can* do for the people you love, using all your capacity. One of those things is preparing for your own death or incapacitation, even though most of us are predisposed to ignore the inevitable (sometimes with a blinding stubbornness).

Leaving healthcare directives for yourself, in case you are unable to make decisions after an accident or illness, is crucial. Equally important is getting legal advice and creating a financial plan that is clear and actionable in the event of your death. Whether you achieve this by leaving a will, creating an insurance policy or giving someone trusted the power of attorney, you owe it to yourself and your loved ones to resolve as many potential issues as possible. Even something as simple as figuring out a plan for your social media accounts, so that your family can cherish your memories after your death, is a great idea.

▪

Grief is one of the heaviest emotions we feel, often leaving people entirely incapacitated when faced with the loss of a loved one. In such moments, they may find themselves simply gliding through the motions, unable to perform even basic tasks. Reducing as much of the decision fatigue as possible can greatly alleviate some of the stress, if not the grief.

In this vein, monetary debts (although crucial) are not the only obligations we carry. The emotional debts you owe your loved ones are often far weightier—the repressed declaration of love you should have made to your untiring, stoic father; the assurance a child should have in your unconditional love; the conviction your friends should have in your unwavering support; the trust your pets should have in your sincerity, even when you are forcing bitter medicines down their throats. While physical injuries may heal and be forgotten, the hidden ones—left behind as the scar tissue from emotional debts—are grave and deep-rooted. And if there is one thing I have learnt from my experience (and the other experiences I subsequently read about) is that your dues and obligations manage to take centre stage, even when you are wrestling with your mortality or are embroiled in a theatrical display of lights, emotions and memories just before an almost-certain death.

This applies to negative feelings too. The more you find yourself struggling to reconcile with your past self and with relationships that have soured, the more you hold yourself back. Ruminating about unresolved issues and unsaid things can weigh you down. In fact, multiple psychologists have narrated instances where clients dwelling on unsaid things about both positive and negative experiences describe a physical tension in their body, manifesting in strained shoulders and necks, headaches and digestive issues. An *NBC News* article mentions, 'Emotional baggage does feel like you are wearing or carrying a bag filled with emotions.'[11]

This weight can contribute to chronic stress and anxiety, and make forming healthy relationships increasingly difficult. It can also lead you to develop self-sabotaging behaviours, as leaving things unsaid automatically robs your best and closest relationships (with friends, partners or family) of the emotional intimacy they deserve.

This is not just important for those brief moments at the end or for some lofty goal about your legacy. Researchers studying the impact of emotional baggage on participants attempting to change their lifestyles reported that: 'Respondents said that they felt that emotional baggage was an important explanation for why they were stuck in old habits and that conversely, being stuck in old habits added load to their already emotional baggage [sic] and made it heavier'.[12]

Unresolved feelings and trauma can weigh you down, make you less productive, and deter you from the goals you have set for yourself. Addressing these feelings is not just an ethical imperative, but a milestone we need to hit for self-improvement. I no longer suppress things. I am aware of the hidden injuries I can cause when interacting with people, and I make a conscious effort to be extremely careful. I have told my mother everything I wished to tell her in those moments on the plane. I have learnt that this is the only way to be at peace with yourself, to achieve a sliver of that real, peaceful calm that you only experience when death lurks just behind the door.

3

GOODNESS

The Triumph of the Human Spirit Amid Chaos

The moment of transcendence I had briefly experienced was like a flash in the dark. It had weight, and it would irrevocably change my life when I awoke, but in that instant, it was over. I was unconscious, still rushing headlong towards a possibly fiery end. I was strapped into my seat, limp and unaware of the chaos unfolding around me. I did not witness the mood in the cabin shift. At some point, the other passengers' curiosity and mild fear about a potential danger lurking boiled over into waves of terror and dread that washed through the cabin. The quiet, imperturbable sea had been stirred; it rose—angry, desperate, loud.

I did not hear the low gasps and exclamations turn into shouts, but Zubair did. 'I remember covering my eyes with the crook of my arm and shoving my head down. I had very quickly gone from being completely calm to being a total wreck. I screamed until the plane came to a halt,' he recalled.[1]

When he finally looked up, he could not see anything. His seat belt was still fastened, but the two seats beside him were gone. He remembers briefly wondering where they had disappeared. Flames had erupted inside the hull, with the aisle and some of the seats engulfed in fire. 'I could not see anyone through the smoke, fire and darkness, but I could hear their screams. They are not something I will easily forget,' he said.

The smoke stung Zubair's eyes and clawed at his throat. He was not on fire, but the heat lashed out at him, assailing his body with the force of something physical. The lack of visibility amplified his fear. Terror grows into something larger when it is accompanied by helplessness. It wracked him most when he thought there was no way out of the darkness, constricting his chest and clouding out everything else for the briefest moment. And then he saw a light behind him.

He unbuckled his seat belt and clambered over the back of his seat into the row behind him. This was the exit row, and he was clawing his way towards the only light he could see. The emergency exit had been flung open, and sunlight was streaming in. He moved through the exit and on to the plane's wing. This was remarkable! The emergency exit is usually near the wing but never on top of it, to allow the crew to deploy the floating inflatable slides that they carry for emergencies like this. The crash had ripped the wing from where it connects to the fuselage and pushed it forward, allowing Zubair to exit the plane and crawl directly on to the wing.

Describing the chaos and confusion he found himself in, he said, 'I moved forward four or five feet on my hands and knees before jumping off the wing and on to the house below. It [the house] had already been destroyed, and for a minute I couldn't figure out how to get out of the rubble. Then I saw a woman emerge from behind a door that was still standing and run towards the exit, and I just followed her out. I don't think she ever saw me.'

Zubair played an active role in getting himself out of danger. He must have experienced a surge of adrenaline. Despite sustaining no internal injuries, he had burns across 31 per cent of his body. He still marvels at this, and is sure that he was never on fire. The burns were a product of the intense heat trapped inside the plane that, unable to escape through the plane's damaged hull, had seared his flesh.

My own escape was much more passive in nature. The change to the aisle seat in the first row (1C) at the time of boarding played a serendipitous but crucial role in my survival. For some reason, when the plane broke apart, a fissure formed near my seat, thrusting it outwards—away from the burning wreckage. I had lost consciousness seconds before the plane nose-dived to the ground and could not attempt an escape.

According to eyewitnesses, my seat fell straight on to a third-floor rooftop instead of the road. Various independent sources have corroborated this. The angle of the fall reduced the damage to my body. The seat then slid off the rooftop and on to the bonnet of a car, instead of landing on the hard asphalt of the road below, further breaking my fall. By then, the plane had crashed into the other end of the street.

By some miracle, the men seated in the car I landed on had been too flabbergasted to react. Although I briefly regained consciousness, I was stuck fast to the seat, now tangled in the car's metal. My back was already burnt, and it was very recently revealed that my spinal cord was also displaced. I do not remember any of this, but I am told that after struggling to free me upon hearing my feeble pleas for help, the men had to call others for assistance.

Meanwhile, Zubair had made his way on to the street. He remembers walking up to a vegetable seller's cart and asking for water. The seller had been busy hawking his produce when the plane crashed. With everyone's attention now riveted to the crash site, he was irritated by Zubair's request, but complied anyway.

What is even more absurd is that Zubair still had his wallet, phone and hard drive on him. Even his sunglasses dangled from his collar. It is not surprising then that when he first told the vegetable seller he had jumped off the plane, the seller thought he was joking and told him not to be dramatic.

When a crowd eventually began to gather and stare at him in awe, Zubair felt his reserves of energy—that had propelled him through the ordeal—finally begin to slip away. He started feeling dizzy and asked the onlookers, who were gathering to take photos and videos, to wait. 'I told them I would take pictures with all of them, but I needed a minute,' he said. But the voyeurism of a local crowd is not so easily contained, and they continued to film him. In one of these clips, he is sitting on the ground in a daze—his shirt unbuttoned, shoes taken off and his sunglasses placed on the ground next to him.

Eventually, locals flagged down an ambulance heading towards the crash, and Zubair was taken to the hospital. While his location on the plane had helped him, Zubair also acted heroically and displayed a remarkable presence of mind in ensuring his survival. He had repeatedly relied on his gut feeling and impulse to move towards safety and somehow managed to follow through in the most terrifying circumstances.

▪

Almost a month after the crash, when I met some of the men who had dragged me to safety, they told me they had seen Zubair sprawled on the ground as they ran towards the narrow street where I lay, enmeshed in the wreckage of the car. They assumed he was a bystander who had been hurt or collapsed in fright.

'I didn't give it much thought,' said Chaudhary Waqas,[2] a property dealer who had been sleeping at his home (just three minutes away from the crash site) when he heard loud voices outside his window. He had looked out to see throngs of people running in the same direction, some shouting about a plane crash.

Several videos uploaded online verify this scene. They show individuals moving towards the thickening coils of black smoke rising into the air in the aftermath of the crash. The people shuffling towards it had their mobile phones raised to record what they were seeing.[3]

Another video, filmed from inside the plane that followed Flight 8303 to Karachi Airport, shows what its passengers saw from their windows—grey plumes of smoke rising from a residential neighbourhood close to the runway, its source unknown. You can even hear someone urge a fellow passenger to look out to the left.[4]

Waqas, too, ran outside and followed the crowd. He walked past Zubair and came to the mouth of a narrow street. The street where the burnt wreckage of the plane lay was a dead end, with the plane blocking the exit. However, building regulations demanded that houses on cul-de-sacs leave small pathways in between to allow pedestrians to access the next street. It was one of these narrow streets that Waqas found himself in. Over time, though, locals had taken possession of these 'escape routes', considering them part of their properties, thereby locking both ends.

Someone shouted for help, 'There's someone stuck under the rubble.' I believe it was one of the passengers of the car I had landed on. The metal gates leading to narrow streets like these were usually padlocked due to security concerns, but on that day, one padlock had been left open. Waqas ran through the narrow street, unsure of what he would find on the other side. He did not have time to think about whether or not this was a good idea, as his feet moved forward as if compelled. He was joined by a few others such as Farhan, Tahir Gujjar and Mohammad Rizwan (who were all locals as well).

Unlike Waqas, who had been woken by the commotion, Rizwan had heard the crash.[5] Born and raised in the area, he knew it like the back of his hand. He supplied milk to most of the neighbourhood and sold the rest from his shop. He had just returned from the Friday prayer and was turning the key in the padlock guarding his shop when a deafening sound ripped through the street.

Rizwan immediately guessed where the sound had come from. Although he had no way of knowing whether it was a plane crash, a bomb or something else entirely, he ran towards that street. The house at the corner of the street belonged to distant relatives—his aunt's sister and her family. He was close enough to get them out.

By the time Rizwan arrived, the family had already jumped from their roof and clambered down to safety on the other side. His attention then turned to the passageway leading to the crash site. Rizwan was one of the first to emerge from the narrow street into the rubble on the other side, but he found himself struggling to see beyond a few feet. 'There was so much smoke, so much fire that I couldn't see a thing,' he said. The intense heat from the burning wreckage slammed into them like an angry, cornered animal. They could still hear screams coming from the direction of the crash.

'It was like a scene from hell,' said Rizwan. 'But we didn't have a way to get near the plane.' If he had relied solely on his sight, he would never have got to me. But by then Rizwan was close enough to hear my strained cries for help. He joined the others gathered around the car to lift me up.

Close on Rizwan's and Waqas' heels, Tahir scrambled through the passage. 'I was one of the last people to reach the car,' he said. 'There were three people ahead of me, and another two or three near the car.'[6]

Tahir had followed the sounds of the children shouting about a plane crashing, and people running towards the street on foot and on bikes. Like Rizwan, he had just returned from the Friday prayer to reopen his bakery and had been standing in front of it when the commotion began. The neighbourhood had been sleepy; Ramadan was coming to an end, and most people had gone home after the prayer. The combination of a month of fasting and the closure of the week had a soporific effect on the streets—unusually quiet and peaceful—before the commotion began.

When Tahir reached the entrance of the narrow passage leading to the crash site, the crowd had begun to figure out that Zubair had been a passenger on the plane. They were surrounding him, asking questions and pulling out their phones to film. But Tahir did not stop to see what was happening. He had seen men disappear down the narrow street and knew someone was in trouble there.

By the time he crossed the street and found himself at the crash site, there were no more screams. All he heard was the sputter and hiss of sparks flying and occasional loud pops, as though someone had lit firecrackers. The black, noxious clouds of smoke that had choked the first two people on the scene did not affect him so much. The smoke was rising straight up now, and Tahir could clearly see me entangled in the wreckage of the car.

'It seemed like something was going to burst,' Tahir said. There was a deep, gnawing feeling in the pit of his stomach that told him they were all standing in an unstable area. Nevertheless, he moved towards the car. I was awake at the time, and saw the men converge towards me. I asked them to lift me gently; my back was burnt and there was a sharp, piercing pain shooting up my leg. My seat belt was still on and my seat had become embedded into the car's wreckage. This is why the people in the car had trouble freeing me on their own. The men who had just arrived on the scene also struggled to pull away debris bit by bit, but eventually managed to pull me free.

Today, they are hard-pressed to remember exactly how they managed to do so. Who cut the seat belt or pulled it loose? Who pried my legs free from the metal cage that had formed around them? Who lifted me up first? None of them remembers the steps they took or the order in which they did so. It is all a frantic, jittery blur for them—a medley of hands pulling, pushing, lifting.

Tahir remembers working amid strange popping noises

that sent shivers down his spine; foreboding sounds that signalled an impending disaster. He was roiling with anxiety as he worked. Waqas too remembers the sharp cracks of the inferno and being blasted dry by an intolerable heat. Rizwan remembers how Army Rangers arrived on the scene, and how he yelled to them for a stretcher. Carrying me through the narrow street that was padlocked on one side and open on the other would have been too hard without a stretcher. The alley was barely wide enough for two people to walk through comfortably; when pedestrians passed through it, they usually ambled through in single file.

A video that surfaced online shortly after the whole ordeal shows five men carrying me away from the Suzuki Cultus I had landed on. I can be seen craning my neck to see where we are going.[7] The road is littered with debris, and a large chunk of the plane that had ripped away from its body lies in the middle of the street; PIA's logo is just barely visible on the side. Nothing is visible behind that chunk—the smoke and fire is too thick to make out anything. A ranger stands behind the men, facing away from the camera, looking directly at the fire. Someone yells in a high and desperate voice, 'Help him, man! Help!' while another voice joins him, 'Nobody is coming this way!' The video then abruptly cuts away.

Eventually, an Edhi Centre[8] ambulance arrived at the other end of the narrow street, and someone brought a stretcher to carry me the rest of the way. They had to tilt the stretcher to pass me over one of the padlocked ends of the street.

Tahir remembers looking back at the red Suzuki just before entering the passage and seeing it go up in flames. A minute and a half earlier, he had been standing on the spot where the fire now raged. He does not know what caused the car to catch fire, but he recalls feeling a wave of relief rolling over him. That feeling of foreboding he had experienced earlier had not been unfounded; they *had* been working in an unstable area, and they had managed to get away with me just in the nick of time.

The next thing I remember is waking up in the hospital. As all this was happening, I dove in and out of consciousness far too many times to construct a linear narrative without the aid of these men who risked their lives to pull me, a complete stranger, out from the jaws of death.

▪

At the time, none of them knew who I was. Rizwan says he only found out I was 'important' later when the news ran stories of my survival. None of them had any monetary incentive to jump into a seething fire to drag me out. No one had needed convincing! They had run largely unbidden towards the sounds of someone struggling.

By the time they dragged me to the ambulance, more authorities had arrived at the scene. Rizwan and Tahir tried to return to the crash site but were told that the area had been cordoned off. This cordoning made sense from the rescuers' points of view. Having untrained civilians trampling through the rubble could have destabilized the area even more, but Rizwan still wonders if they could have saved someone else if they had been allowed back.

The lengths to which they went to help me confounded me in the beginning. I was never a cynical man, but I had not expected such a deluge of selfless acts. It was humbling to get a glimpse of the inherent goodness in people. I wondered when we had collectively decided that the masses were 'hard to control' during crises of this nature. Why do we assume the presence of greed and reduce the average man to a selfish, chaotic mess when designing policies to cater to natural disasters?

Freie explores exactly this in his fascinating book about the culture of death. He looks at several disasters, like Hurricane Katrina, the Japanese tsunami of 2011 and the 1906 San Francisco earthquake to see how the masses respond to large-scale disasters and how the elite view them. Unsurprisingly, the elite tend to see disasters as 'challenges to order, viewing the masses as irrational, panic-prone, and likely to loot and even murder'.[9]

One does not need to look too far in Pakistan to begin to empathize with this view and go down a dark rabbit hole of collective self-loathing. In a country divided along religious, ethnic and political lines, mob mentality has repeatedly taken centre stage. In December 2021, a Sri Lankan factory manager was beaten to death and burnt by a mob following allegations of 'blasphemy'—a virulently incendiary topic in radical circles.[10] In another incident, in August 2023, an enraged mob of radicals vandalized and burnt multiple churches in Faisalabad and attacked Christian homes after local Christians were accused of burning the Holy Quran.

Pakistan has always struggled to control mobs; several women have been assaulted by mobs on multiple occasions, and roads and transportation networks grind to a halt any time there is a protest (which often devolves into violence).

But there is also another side to Pakistan. Every time a natural disaster has hit the country, citizens have come together to offer help. While this does not right the wrongs committed by mobs, it does offer an insight into Freie's contentions about the misperceptions the elite tend to cultivate about the general public.

In and after disasters, ordinary people tend to offer their assistance and cooperate with each other. My experiences after the crash are also certainly indicative of the inherent goodness in people. It is hard for me to then take long-winded theories about man's innate 'villainy' seriously, but it is amusing to dissect them.

▪

Freie's critique of the 'elite' works surprisingly well as a critique of many established philosophers grappling with the nature of humanity. Thomas Hobbes saw peace as a rare and fragile achievement, painstakingly wrought by a sovereign or authoritative body that was able to enforce laws and resolve conflicts.[11] According to him, any type of anarchy or dissent would lead back to man's real nature—brutish and ugly. Other philosophers, like Jean-Jacques Rousseau, had less pessimistic views. For Rousseau, humankind was naturally good until it was corrupted by the greed that unequal societies produced.[12]

Philosophers across the world have wrestled with these ideas. Chinese Confucianism, especially post-Song dynasty (960–1279), also revolved around mankind's inherent nature. According to some Confucian philosophers, men were essentially good. Mencius argued that men's sense of compassion developed into benevolence, their sense of shame and disdain developed into righteousness, their sense of respect developed into propriety, and their sense of right and wrong developed into wisdom. If individuals became bad, it was not because of their inherent nature but because their innate senses had not been developed properly.[13]

In contrast, Xunzi saw men as inherently bad, who had to cultivate their moral sense through learning. Meanwhile, the Chinese legalists perceived humans primarily as selfish beings, whose selfishness could be used by the state to enforce order by creating a system of incentives.[14]

Other philosophers, like John Locke, argued that we are born with minds that are *tabula rasa* (Latin for 'a blank slate'), and that sensory experiences fashion us into who we are and give us rules for processing data.[15] More modern thinkers like David L. Hull have argued that there is no set of intrinsic traits universal among humans, and that any kind of 'sameness' is purely accidental and temporary from a biological standpoint.[16]

And so, philosophers and political scientists, freethinkers

and advocates of different states have gone round and round in circles trying to pinpoint the exact nature of man. (Unsurprisingly, for most of human history, these debates were largely preoccupied with the inherent nature of the male gender; women were relegated to inconsequential roles.) You can tie yourself up in knots thinking about which side presents more compelling arguments. In a lot of ways, all these philosophies are products of their times. We tend to see our lives as 'nasty, brutish and short' when civil war abounds, while our views become more sympathetic and forgiving during peaceful times.

Interestingly, just as most collective artistic representations of NDEs tend to veer towards the hellish, works of art that deal with humankind's inherent nature also tend to vilify humans. That is probably because vilifying makes things more entertaining, even though I cannot help but think that it also makes us more pessimistic.

Take, for example, *Lord of the Flies*—William Golding's novel about a group of young boys stranded on an uninhabited island and their attempts to form a makeshift society. In Golding's dystopian world, the boys form rules and regulations that are meant to help them all survive, ascribing power to totems and dividing duties like hunting and gathering. But order quickly devolves into chaos when the spectre of a 'beast' emerges; the boys turn on each other, resorting to sadistic acts of violence and killing the weaker among them.

As their society disintegrates around them, the more perceptive of the boys begin to realize that there is no beast.

'Maybe there is a beast … maybe it's only us,' thinks one of the seminal characters, in one of the most quoted lines from the book.[17] There is a darkness lurking in their hearts, and they must fear their own natures more than some make-believe sea monster. Eventually, British naval officers rescue them, and the sight of a uniformed adult jolts the boys out of their savage state of mind.

The book quickly became a classic and is still taught in schools today. Golding wrote the book after reading *The Coral Island* by R.M. Ballantyne, which he believed had unrealistically positive portrayals of children. He wanted to write a book about what would *really* happen if kids found themselves on an island without adult supervision, given how nonchalantly cruel children can be.[18] His remains one of the most pessimistic views of human nature in literature today, given that it deals with children—the one group that even most mainstream literature portrays as innocent and naïve.

However, Golding's portrayal may not be as 'realistic' as he claims. In 1965, a group of young boys did find themselves in a situation similar to that of Golding's novel, but their reactions were far from savage.[19] Sick of their school meals and bored of their little school, the six boys had decided to take a boat out to sea and go to Fiji, maybe even New Zealand. During the first night, all of them went to sleep and their little boat drifted off course. They spent eight days drifting on a merciless ocean, until they found the island of 'Ata, a rocky island near Tonga in the Pacific Ocean, and set up camp there. An Australian captain found them after they were marooned for more than a year. During the 15 months they were lost, funerals were held and they were given up for dead. According to Rutger Bregman,

> [...] 'the boys had set up a small commune with food garden, hollowed-out tree trunks to store rainwater, a gymnasium with curious weights, a badminton court, chicken pens and a permanent fire, all from handiwork, an old knife blade and much determination.' While the boys in *Lord of the Flies* come to blows over the fire, those in this real-life version tended their flame so it never went out, for more than a year.[20]

They discovered wild crops, made musical instruments and survived thirst and even nursed a broken leg. In a hilarious setback, when they finally reached a town, they were all promptly arrested for stealing the boat that had taken them out to sea. Eventually, all of them made it back to their hometown safe and healthy. Years later, when a writer approached the man who rescued them, he handed over his memoir. 'Life has taught me a great deal,' it began, 'including the lesson that you should always look for what is good and positive in people.'[21]

▪

After everything I have experienced, I have come to the realization that perhaps we enjoy consuming media and literature that play on man's vile nature because they are exciting. But when it comes down to it, people are generally good. Despite the overall societal decay I have witnessed in my lifetime, I am forever inclined to believe in this goodness. After all, I remain indebted to the men who pulled me out of the wreckage and got me medical help. I also know that my experiences are not unique.

In the aftermath of the magnitude 7.6 earthquake in northern Pakistan in 2005, which claimed 80,000 lives and left around 4 million homeless, Pakistani citizens got together to form elaborate chains to transport funds, blankets, food and clothes to the north.[22] Donations also poured in from around the world. Volunteers helped clear roads to reach isolated communities in the mountains, and medics and doctors volunteered their time. After flash floods ravaged small nomadic communities and villages in southern Pakistan in 2010, affecting almost 20 million people, a similar influx of donations poured in.

This spirit of organized collaboration certainly validates Freie's claims, which is why the assumption that people are prone to mass hysteria and crime can often have tragic consequences. As Freie mentions, 'The cultural interpretation that the danger of disasters is to be found in mass panic—and therefore elite control is necessary—can be extended to individual dying experiences where elites are more concerned with control than developing policies sensitive to humane dying experiences.'[23]

Like Freie, I believe that our policies would be much more humane if our ruling elite internalized the idea that the masses are generally good, and not just when it comes to healthcare for the terminally ill. This kind of thinking leads to a very narrow range of ideas and policies that are considered acceptable or mainstream within a given societal and political context. In other words, it forms a very narrow Overton Window.[24] Rethinking policymaking from a place of compassion, expanding the ambit of palatable policies, and forming what can only be described as a charter of society would greatly improve federal policies.

If businesses promoted a culture of compassion, they would not only see a reduction in employees' stress levels but would also benefit from the improved work ethics and culture. A survey conducted in Canada from 2000 to 2008 found that healthcare costs at organizations that put their employees through the ringer were 46 per cent higher than those at organizations with lower stress levels.[25] Meanwhile, employees with better moods and better workplace relationships tend to be more productive and loyal to their organizations.[26]

It is a shame, then, that so many organizations have adopted the stance that compassionate leadership and business practices might make leaders appear weak, especially in the face of so much evidence to the contrary. The most beloved leaders of the 20th and 21st centuries—Desmond Tutu, Nelson Mandela, Abdul Sattar Edhi—led their movements and organizations primarily from a place of compassion.

At an intellectual level, I always understood the benefits of compassionate leadership, but it was not until I was confronted with the goodness of people time and again after my crash that I truly grasped it on a deeper level. I believe in management by empathy, which is one of the reasons I have tried to create a healthier environment for employees in every organization I have headed, not just in general but also specifically for underprivileged groups. In one of the largest hiring campaigns at the BOP in 2021, we began a drive to hire more women at equal pay. I recognize the resentment and inequality that stems from gender biases in this country and refuse to let that dictate my organization's culture.

Even though the corporate sector in Pakistan is miles ahead of many others when it comes to correcting gender biases, there is still a long way to go. In banking, for instance, there are still many conventions I would like to change. For example, women are often facilitated when applying for loans or mortgages on their own. However, following one of the oddest policies in the Pakistani banking system, two brothers can apply for a joint mortgage whereas two sisters cannot. The reasoning behind this is that women do not have complete agency when making financial decisions after they are married. This line is parroted by mortgage officials and bankers with a matter-of-fact nonchalance. There is very little awareness that it reaffirms sexist views about gender roles and perpetuates them further by reducing the ambit of financial opportunities available to women.

However, if something as simple as transparency can make parity more achievable in the corporate world, and help fight decades of internalized biases against one gender, then it is hard not to believe in the goodness of people. I try to encourage the same at the BOP. In fact, the bank has taken concrete steps to assist many underprivileged groups in this way, not just women. For instance, we have introduced refinancing schemes for special persons, empowering them to set up or expand business ventures. This parity and inclusion in social and financial circles is essential for a better society and community. By fostering a culture where honesty and accountability are prized above all else—and employees know that management trusts in their goodness—I believe we can change toxic or draining work cultures for the better.

I also see a shift in the collective consciousness when I observe the demands the general population worldwide has for big corporations. As information has become more easily available, people around the world have rallied to demand accountability from them. For instance, it is no longer easy for large companies to brush off concerns about climate, their working conditions, or exploitation of child labour or engaging in animal abuse. And while there are still many horrifying practices that need to come to an end, the growing movement for corporate accountability gives me hope for humanity.

This is why the assumption that the general public lacks goodness, and must be manipulated by appeals to their selfish nature, is now an obsolete marketing strategy. Unlike the cynical approach that marketing gurus sometimes take (think the wildly popular series *Mad Men*, in which a creative director at a marketing agency finds novel ways of spinning creative lies about products), I believe that this myopic understanding of marketing may lead budding marketers to forgo moral scruples and consideration of virtue in exchange for lead generation and sales. This understanding is short-sighted; with increasingly perceptive audiences, strategies that rely on manipulation—rather than truth and goodness—damage a brand's story and perception.

Losses that result from neglecting ethical considerations are severe and far-reaching. In a world where compliance no longer rests with quality-assurance individuals alone but also with the marketers who create the narratives around products, it is imperative (and also profitable) for brands to be seen as creating a difference and making informed decisions. Campaigns that prioritize ethics also age better. For instance, fast fashion—cheap, low-quality clothing produced under exploitative conditions—is increasingly falling out of favour. Consumers are gravitating towards responsibly produced options, even at higher prices, as they seek to avoid contributing to child labour in South Asia. Similarly, fashion brands are moving away from homogeneous and 'white' ideals of beauty, celebrating diversity in body types and races.

Disingenuous messaging is no longer palatable. While global audiences will always have conflicting interests and values, it is no longer adequate for firms to produce quality products while remaining neutral on key social and ethical issues. Firms must now make moral decisions about their operations, working conditions, target markets, etc. They must appeal to the inherent goodness in people, from a place of moral corporate responsibility, even when the alternative seems more profitable. Just as governments cannot haughtily assume that people are driven only by their own selfish needs, companies cannot assume that either. And individuals like you and I cannot fall prey to the cynicism perpetuated by contemporary media narratives that portray humans as inherently bad.

▪

For me, these introspective thoughts came as a result of an NDE and the subsequent assistance I received from hundreds of people, and it has made me a happier and more fulfilled person. I was dragged out of an extremely volatile situation while drifting in and out of consciousness by a group of people who had no way of knowing who I was—and who could not possibly have harboured any ulterior motives. In the days following the crash, complete strangers reached out to me with outpourings of love and helped me recover.

When I first reached the hospital and gained the wherewithal to begin to look at my surroundings, I noticed that dozens of people genuinely concerned about my well-being had shown up. This was not because I led a life free of conflict—I had had a very tense relationship with the employee union at National Savings in the Ministry of Finance. But these people—who had previously carried out protests against me and had even filed an unsuccessful case against my appointment in court—were the first ones to arrive at the hospital and offer all kinds of assistance, including blood donations.

This was a shock to me. In my brief spell at National Savings, I had joined with an eye towards casting off the lethargy and challenging the mediocrity that can sometimes develop in government departments with airtight job security. I had begun to make the department more performance-driven and delivery-oriented, a move that was not accepted by the employees. Those who could have previously coasted through their jobs at the department until retirement now felt their job security was under threat, and the labour union began resisting the changes I was suggesting.

Since they were driven by fear of what they saw as a potentially ruthless management style, the protests gained steam very quickly. The union organized a protest outside my office. This was right before the 2018 elections in Pakistan, and as political parties began to see that including the issue in their electoral platforms would give them more clout, several political leaders also began to show up at these protests to make speeches—one of whom later became the Minister of Finance after the election.

For well over a month, I walked through an active protest and, at times, a belligerent mob to get to my office at the ministry. A month before my contract was up for renewal, I decided not to extend it. The resistance to change had reached toxic proportions, and I wanted peace of mind and the potential for growth—neither of which seemed possible if I stayed. Once I made the decision public, the protests dissipated. Perhaps this also partially explains why I was hesitant to take on the leadership role at the BOP; I had preconceived notions about the inertia that can build up in government departments. Thankfully, I was wrong on that front.

Given how hostile my stint at National Savings had become, I was shocked to see colleagues from the Ministry show up at the hospital, asking after me with genuine concern plastered all over their faces. These selfless overtures from many ex-colleagues firmed up my faith in humanity. But you should not wait for an equally calamitous event to peel back the hardened layers of pessimism you may have wrapped yourself in. Expect the best from people and give your best in return; harness the power of optimism, and you will see your life become simpler, happier and more magical.

Almost a month after the crash, as soon as I was able to leave the hospital bed, I met the men who had saved me in Karachi. I was floored not just by their bravery but also by their personal struggles in the aftermath. They had witnessed something horrific and were coping with it on their own. Rizwan remembers how difficult it became for him to talk about the crash because people were still curious, and news reporters kept asking questions—picking at the scabs of the memories he was trying so hard to repress. Waqas says he still jumps into situations where he can offer help, but for a year after the crash, he would break into a cold sweat whenever he thought about it. Tahir had to actively avoid people who came to Model Colony looking for my rescuers, hoping to be introduced to me in the hope of financial assistance from a bank president they had never met. He shudders at the memories of the rescue, at the closeness of the fire that erupted moments after they lifted me away.

In the days after the crash, as rescue workers swarmed the area, local politicians and community leaders ensured that the residents of Model Colony whose houses had been damaged had food, water and shelter, Tahir recalls. The celebratory atmosphere that had preceded the crash in anticipation of Eid was swept away by what the locals had seen. One of the deaths was that of a child who had been unable to escape the conflagration after the plane crashed. While all the other residents escaped with mere bruises, grief, fear and paranoia still gripped their hearts. Tahir's account makes me wonder how many residents of Model Colony—whom we considered 'adjacent' to the crash—had had their lives upended because of it.

These people had witnessed the first few moments after the crash. They had rushed through the chaos even before uniformed personnel had shown up to demarcate safe zones and chart a plan of action. They had seen hell, and they remembered it. Sometimes it reared its ugly head on sleepless nights and slow mornings, but none of them regret what they had done. I will forever be indebted to their spirit and bravery, and consider myself changed because of it.

4

SINCERITY

A Gruelling Rescue and a Desperate Search for Answers

Mohammad Bilal, the head of Edhi's Ambulance Control Services, was in the control room when he first heard about the crash. Bilal is a seasoned veteran of the rescue staff. He has worked with Edhi for almost 30 years and has pulled people out of the wrecks of car accidents, shuttled them to hospitals during brutal heat waves, and staunched their blood. He has also ferried victims of politically motivated shootings in his fleet of ambulances. He has the weathered, calm look that is common to emergency personnel in large conurbations— weighed down by the number of people they have to serve and the relative frequency of incidents compared to smaller, rural areas. Cynical but self-assured.

'*Haadse batake nahin aate*', he repeated a phrase several

times when recounting the crash, 'Accidents don't announce themselves before arriving.[1] His years of experience had taught him two things: no one was ever prepared for an event of this nature, and that swiftness was key.

As soon as Bilal heard about the crash, he made a quick calculation in his head. Of all the ambulance checkpoints in the area, the Malir and Stargate centres would have the shortest routes to the crash site. Stargate would have multiple ambulances available. It would take them between 10 and 15 minutes to reach the burning husk of the plane in Model Colony, whether they took the route that ran adjacent to the airport or the wider Shahrah-e-Faisal that ran through the heart of the city. Meanwhile, the ambulances from Malir could pass through the army cantonment area and reach the site in 6 to 9 minutes. That road would not pass for a calm street in a small town but compared to the chaos of Shahrah-e-Faisal—which converges into the National Highway and is widely considered Karachi's deadliest road—it would be easier.

Still, he dispatched vehicles from both centres, fervently hoping that the post-prayer traffic would not slow them down as they sped along their routes. Then he spoke to the remaining staff in these two locations. The plane crash would require all hands on deck, he told them. They were in for some long days and nights.

By the time Bilal got to the crash site, half an hour had elapsed. The smoke around the entrance of the narrow street had cleared somewhat, and Zubair and I had already been hauled away by the ambulances he had sent earlier. He could see rubble stretching in all directions. The fire in the plane was still raging. It would go on for another two hours. Unlike the people who had pulled me out, Bilal heard nothing—just an overbearing silence from the body of the plane, and the sounds of the rescuers yelling directions and their equipment clanging across the paths they were making.

The heat from the blaze inside the plane was still harsh. It made his eyes water. The acrid smoke that rose from its direction was sending many rescuers around him into coughing fits. It was still too hot and too unstable to approach, but rangers and firemen were working on getting closer, and the fires outside the plane had been largely extinguished.

Bilal looked around and saw that there were others who had been ejected from the aircraft, when cracks and fissures had torn across its hull during the descent. Being thrown out of the plane alone had not saved my life. I was thrown fast, and the seat I was strapped into had provided some cushioning during the fall. Bilal remembers recovering six or seven bodies from the rooftops around the plane—all burnt beyond recognition. They were still so hot to the touch that the white surgical gloves he wore began to melt and stick to the tips of his fingers and palms. He asked his colleagues to bring cotton gloves, his voice hoarse with both urgency and smoke. He wrapped cotton sheets around the remains of the victims so that he could handle them.

He had seen this kind of a fiery event once before, when buses on the Kohistan Super Highway had caught fire after colliding with cars carrying fuel tanks. The gas cylinders on board had exploded, and the passengers had been burnt to a crisp. Fire in a contained space can be as intense as an explosion, with heat rising to unfathomable levels. Bilal recalled that the smell of the crash site brought those memories bubbling to the surface. Still, he worked quickly, methodically. Around him, the firemen and rangers had begun to hack at the body of the plane—cutting away large chunks to access the people inside.

A pall hung in the air. Bilal estimates that there were 40 or 50 rescue workers from the Edhi Foundation on the scene. Similarly, large numbers of rangers, firemen and volunteers from the Chhipa Welfare Association were also present. Every single person understood that they would not find anyone alive, but they dug with a desperate haste. In some ways, the fire had shortened the suffering of those inside, but this would be no consolation to the families waiting for their loved ones.

▪

I look at the post-crash pictures of this neighbourhood now, and I marvel at these events. In these images, the narrow streets of Model Colony are in a flurry of confusion. It looks like the site of a bomb blast or an earthquake. Some houses have lost their entire façades, whilst others have no roofs. Even the ones that remain standing are singed black by the flames that spread through the area, ravaging cars and buildings. I have since learnt that many of these buildings violated building codes. In a city as overpopulated as Karachi, teeming with millions of migrants, owners of residential buildings often tack on an additional floor to lease out or to cater to their burgeoning families. High-rise commercial buildings do the same, and those in Model Colony were no different. Perhaps, if these buildings had been lower, the plane would have made it to a clear stretch of land before it crashed. But in the crowded residential street, it wrought even more havoc. Those images show shattered glass and debris lying everywhere, and officials in military uniforms move through the debris with calculated movements.

As seen in the images, in the most congested places—where the steaming wreck of the plane lies—there is no room to move. There only remains a charred mess that looks unsalvageable, a tangled mess of concrete, structural iron bent at hideous angles, and wires. Large hunks of metal from the plane lie in odd shapes across the street, some rest upright against the buildings. In one photo, two rescue officials inspect a street full of rubble, while a large group of rangers stand in the back. The only thing one can identify is a semi-crushed turbine engine lying in a corner.[2]

In another image, fire department officials stand on the roof of a building (that is only partially intact) and shoot down a jet of water into the street below.[3] There is no room for fire trucks and rescue equipment. Bilal remembers those thick streams of water attempting to extinguish the flames, sizzling over charred and blackened rubble that hissed angrily under the force. The flames soon began to sputter and die.

As the rescuers began to cut away the plane, Bilal's army of volunteers also began to somewhat organize the rescue efforts. The tiny, 1.5- to 2-ft-wide street that led to the road where the plane had crashed was not wide enough for the traffic of volunteers, emergency personnel, stretchers and body bags that were moving through it. Bilal and some of the other volunteers began to widen the path by knocking down a wall and clearing the way to the plane.

Some could smell their own hair smouldering or feel cinders landing on their exposed flesh as they worked—little lightning strikes that made them wince. Others had purple welts on their arms, bruises from falling detritus as walls were knocked down and the debris shifted. But through the mesh of wire and metal, a path slowly emerged for the other personnel to follow.

Over the next few hours, firefighters and volunteers repeated the same laborious manoeuvres. They drilled, sawed and cut away parts of the plane, recovered the people closest to these parts, then cut away some more. Sweat began to drench their clothes. For some, the sweat was a welcome respite, since even the tiniest breeze would help now. At times, they had to wait for the plane to cool down before attempting to remove the bodies inside. Not all were recovered whole, but that is something Bilal does not dwell on.

Post-crash investigations showed how complete the decimation was. The cockpit, nose landing gear, an MCG wheel, one of the engines and the left-hand-side wing, another wing tip, and flap fairings[4] were found on rooftops around the street. The rest of the plane lay in pieces on the ground. Tahir and Rizwan had heeded the rescue workers and returned to their shops. 'It was beyond our capability to do anything just then,' said Tahir. 'And the rangers would not have let us return to the crash site anyway.'

Waqas, who claims to be involved in the rescue efforts after the officials arrived, says that those days left an indelible mark on him. He describes limbs discovered and bodies cut open in gruesome detail. His recollections seem like an attempt to make sense of something he had witnessed, rather than a morbid focus on sensational details. For weeks after the crash, he says he chased away people who had come to the crash site to indulge their meaner, prying natures. In his own words, 'The area was cordoned off, but the rescue workers heading in and out were usually surrounded by large throngs of people, who travelled from interior Sindh, from Hyderabad, to see the site of the crash. They were getting in the way, but they didn't care.'

Many assumed Waqas was more approachable than other locals because he was a real estate agent who gave tours of houses in the area. They did not realize that he was just as offended by this fascination with the macabre as the other residents of Model Colony. The area became a site for what can only be described as disaster tourism; an idea most of us generally attribute to rich Westerners. At least in that case, the vast majority of tourists visit disaster sites decades or centuries after the event. They throng to

Pompeii to see a city burnt by volcanic ash in AD 79, or to the sites of the Holocaust during the Second World War to pay their respects to the deceased. However, this immediate, all-consuming curiosity about a tragedy that had just occurred and whose victims had not even been buried was something many residents of Model Colony found disrespectful and predatory, almost sacrilegious.

Once again, I was hit by how the crash affected even those that were not victims and their families. How many now looked at air travel with a creeping sense of dread? How many had rushed to the scene, but now lay awake at night replaying the horrors they had witnessed as bystanders? And who was responsible for their suffering?

▪

While the immediate rescue efforts to recover the 98 victims from the crash site were laudable, our country's systems and infrastructure were not equipped to deal with a disaster of this scale. Once the remains of the victims had been recovered, there was a flurry of disorganized activities in the hospitals they were headed to. Bilal describes how the mortuaries in Jinnah Hospital and Civil Hospital ran out of space. The victims were shuttled to multiple locations. Given the unrecognizable state of the remains, there was no way to keep track of who had gone where. Eventually, many of the victims were moved to the Edhi mortuary. It took between 12 and 36 hours to process this intake. The relatives of the victims went from location to location seeking information.

Some of their loved ones could only be identified through DNA testing, a process complicated further by the number of places that the victims were being kept in. Their stories were heart-rending.

The process became murky, slow and bureaucratic. The victims' families reeled between grief and anger. In one case, the body of 14-year-old Ibrahim Polani was handed over to the wrong family, who was also looking for a child wearing braces. I had known the family for most of my life. Ibrahim's grandfather, Zakariya Polani, was a close friend of my father's from Lahore. Ibrahim's father Zain had been like a sibling to me. He was the same age as my youngest brother, Ali. Before the crash, I did not know they were on the flight with me. I only learnt of this later when I was in the hospital. In a tragic turn of events, Ibrahim's siblings and parents had also perished in the crash, and had been buried by the family whilst they waited to recover Ibrahim. By the time the authorities figured out their mistake, the boy had been buried in a different graveyard by the family who took him home thinking they had found their daughter.[5]

Meanwhile, some family members began to question the ethics and disaster management practices of the airline itself. They questioned how PIA could continue to make profits while holding hostage the compensation meant for the families.[6]

Relatives of the crash victims began to protest, gathering outside the Karachi Press Club, holding up pictures of the people they had lost. Some alleged that the airline was also withholding insurance money, and that the aviation ministry needed to take action against the PCAA and PIA. Some PIA officials claimed that all funds would eventually be disbursed. The families' anger was justifiable. I cannot begin to fathom the extent of their losses, nor presume to describe them. Back then, I was struggling with my own demons and could not bring myself to face the bereft.

As someone who needs to travel frequently for work and family, I was focused entirely on making sure that there were no residual dregs of fear left in my body. I made it a point to take the same flight back to Lahore, and to sit in the same seat. Other than a momentary flicker of panic when the plane began to land, I remained calm throughout the flight. As I write this, I realize that while it is imperative to have faith and to not let tragedy define you, it is also equally important for airlines to ensure that their passengers' faith does not just stem from their own strength of character, but from a trust in the airline's ability to keep them safe.

At a time when information was limited, transparency would have been key, but multiple authorities had created a bureaucratic tangle and organizational mess that left these families without closure, and without the capacity to fully grieve.

Even with constrained resources and limited fiscal space, processing the remains of the dead could have been handled tactfully. It may have made it less painful if the details of the investigations had been sincerely communicated to the people who had spent interminable hours and days searching for their families, without an end in sight. This lack of transparency pitted these families not just against the administrative staff but also against the rescue workers who had tirelessly recovered everyone.

The rightful anger and desperation that the families felt, combined with the sensationalized media coverage of the crash, had the effect of lumping all authorities together in conversations about the crash. My decision to fly with the airline again to assuage my fears added fuel to the fire. In retrospect, I admit that I had been focused on my recovery, and had not thought of how this would appear to others. Meanwhile, rescue workers found themselves being painted with the same brush as the administrative staff that was guilty of negligence and incompetence.

In the aftermath of tragedies like this one, if people in charge are perceived to be 'spinning the truth' or focusing on public relations rather than action, the blowback is usually amplified by pain. Across history, governments or local administrative authorities have often cited the excuse that sincerity can lead to chaos in times of crisis, but this seems like an infantilization of the masses on par with the idea discussed earlier in the book—that they will act violently and greedily in the aftermath of disasters. Even well-meaning authorities engaged in obfuscation of the truth may seem akin to people who spin the truth to accumulate power or wealth, or some other highly prized resource.

▪

So, how sincere should people in positions of power be? This is a question I have asked myself multiple times since the crash. I understand the authorities' pragmatism that tempers the flow of information when things seem chaotic, but the cost of pulling a veil over everything until the disaster has been managed also seems too high.

Over the years, many philosophers have looked at the concept of sincerity from a variety of angles—some have struggled to pin down its exact nature, while others have debated its usefulness. Some purists, in their rigid adherence to elevated principles, have argued for a degree of sincerity others have found unrealistic. Immanuel Kant, for instance, argued that lying was so abhorrent an activity that if a murderer showed up at your door and enquired about the location of your friend, with the intent to kill said friend, you should tell him the truth.[7]

Of course, this rigidity has been ridiculed by subsequent philosophers; Kant's severity does not make sense in an imperfect world. By his argument, some have said, those who harboured Jews during the Nazi holocaust of the Second World War should have turned over the refugees they hid in their basements and cellars to the genocidal army of Hitler. Others claim this is too simplistic an understanding of the ideas Kant proposed.

For the most part though, sincerity as a concept has been rigorously examined in the context of politics. Fitting perhaps, since that is the field where it is severely lacking. Across empires and regimes, politicians (and those who seek to benefit from them) have moulded popular narratives without regard to truth or sincerity.

This dishonesty is perhaps expected when it comes to straightforward matters of policy or political rivalry. However, it also has a profound, lasting impact on the stories that we tell ourselves about our collective history and the long-held narratives that nations cling to.

Consider the 1857 war of independence in undivided India. For Indians—Hindus, Sikhs and Muslims alike—it was the War of Independence. For the British EIC, which functioned as a sovereign power on behalf of the increasingly colonial and ambitious British Crown, it was 'mutiny'. This distinction alone sufficiently explains the narratives that were created around this war.

The war was precipitated by a number of issues, including culturally insensitive social reforms by the EIC, harsh land taxes and general mistreatment. While the rebels were able to capture large tracts of land in Awadh and the North-West Frontier Province, they were quickly beaten back by the British forces. Provinces like Punjab and Bengal remained largely neutral, and after several bloody and brutal spats of violence perpetrated by both sides in the affected provinces, the British troops wrested back control of these areas. This war had a profound impact on the way the British operated in India. In its aftermath, the British passed the Government of India Act in 1858, reorganizing India's administration and financial set-up, and dissolving the EIC's powers in favour of direct British rule.

It is not surprising, then, that the war was painted

in such starkly different ways by the British and Indian contemporaries of the time. History is usually written by the victors, and several decades later historians are still plumbing the depths of the insincerity of the colonial government in India to dig up more accurate historical accounts.

One such account is that of Havildar (Sergeant) Alum Bheg of the 46th Regiment of the Bengal Native Infantry (BNI). Bheg was involved in the rebellion at Sialkot in 1857, an event that is largely overlooked by many historians. In 1963, Bheg's skull was discovered in a pub in Kent, England, with the following note: 'Skull of Havildar "Alum Bheg," 46th Regt. Bengal N. Infantry who was *blown away from a gun* [...]. He was a principal leader in the mutiny of 1857 & of a most ruffianly disposition.'[8]

It went on to vilify Bheg as a murderer of Europeans. A British officer, Captain Costello, who had been present at Bheg's execution, had collected the skull as a grisly trophy of war. It had then travelled across oceans and continents to land in the reluctant hands of a pub owner who did not know what to do with it, and who eventually handed it to Kim Wagner—a researcher who studied this era of British history.

In a book that recreates Bheg's life from the accounts of Europeans, and those that worked with the 46th BNI, Wagner painstakingly put together the story of the war. While Indian soldiers had engaged in violent assaults in other parts of the country, Wagner found that in Sialkot they had remained calm until they heard that the British intended to disarm them to prevent mutiny. In essence, the stories of brutality on the part of Indian soldiers in Sialkot are overblown and exaggerated to justify the horrific British retaliation. Wagner writes:

> The truth was that the outbreak at Sialkot was a highly contingent and confusing event, and one that in many ways differed from the mutinies that had taken place earlier that year at Meerut, Delhi and elsewhere. At Sialkot, there were [...] no random lynching of isolated *sahibs*, no sexual attacks on *memsahibs* and no mutilation of their corpses. There had been numerous opportunities for *sepoys* and other locals [...] should they so have wished, but it never happened.[9]

Painting all rebels with the same brush was a political decision, not a sincere one. To deter hot-headed rebels from attempting something similar in the future, the British levied horrifying punishments with dizzying speed. Further, to justify these punishments, they pushed the narrative that *all* rebels had been brutish and violent. What this meant for soldiers like Alum Bheg was a death that horrified the Indians. When he was eventually captured, his body was strapped to a cannon and blown to smithereens to ensure that there would not be enough of him left for his funeral rites or burial. Whilst many, including Wagner, have proposed that Bheg's skull be repatriated to his home country for burial near the river Ravi, it remains in the UK.[10]

As in all narratives of war or conflict written by victors,

in the story of Alum Bheg, the political elite sacrificed sincerity at the altar of duplicity. This story is far from the only historical account that has been corrupted to serve a political agenda. What is even more interesting, and perhaps nefarious, is the fact that we continue to engage in such obfuscation of facts in our history books, popular culture and media.

For instance, Indians and Pakistanis often see Winston Churchill—the British prime minister who led his country to victory in the Second World War—in a very different light compared to the British. For the UK, Churchill towers over everyone as a paragon of reason. His fame as a great strategist and adviser to the Queen has only grown since his time. Some contemporary TV shows, such as *The Crown*, continue to apotheosize the man, while others like *Peaky Blinders* portray a man with more nefarious plans.

Indians and Pakistanis have a very different collective memory of the man. Whilst his indefatigable work and policies may have led a war-torn England to freedom and recovery, his strength of conviction and patriotism was a death-knell for British-controlled India. In 1943, the Bengal province (present-day Bangladesh, West Bengal and eastern India) experienced famine on an unprecedented scale. According to recent historians who have examined rainfall data from that time period, this famine was not brought about by drought but by policy failure. Amartya Sen, the Indian-born economist and Nobel laureate, argued in 1981 that the deaths of close to 3 million people had happened because of 'wartime inflation, speculative buying and panic hoarding'.[11] Journalist Madhusree Mukerjee takes this one step further, and argues that 'the famine was exacerbated by the decisions of Winston Churchill's wartime cabinet in London'.[12]

Churchill's wartime cabinet was repeatedly warned not to export rice from India to the rest of the empire for the war effort, but they continued to do so. While India's then viceroy was pleading for an emergency stock of 1 million tonnes of wheat to alleviate the famine in Bengal, British forces continued to remove rice stocks from the country. Churchill blamed the Indians for 'breeding like rabbits', and even questioned the severity of the shortages by reportedly asking why Mahatma Gandhi was still alive if the situation was so terrible.

Britain also engaged in a 'denial policy'—confiscating supplies of rice and thousands of boats from Bengal's coastline to ensure that they did not fall into Japanese hands.

It is clear that while Churchill's strategies led the British to victory, his legacy is one that is tainted by the blood of millions of Indians. Yet, this dark chapter of history is hardly, if ever, taught in British schools or portrayed in British films and TV shows.

This 'whitewashing' of history—a deliberate, slow and insidious rewriting of facts and political discourse—is an old tactic, and it proves one thing: once sincerity is sacrificed, for political gain or simplicity, it becomes very hard to recover the truth. Cicero urged politicians to make sincerity a cornerstone of their character.[13] Today, I understand that this sincerity is important not only for your own personal moral record but also because the smallest act of insincerity can affect collective histories, ideologies and the collective trauma that societies carry as a result.

It also means that there are implications for how people perceive authorities who are less than sincere today. Since insincerity in disseminating information has historically been a tactic used for political gain, the authorities withholding information today can easily be mistaken for power-hungry or corrupt individuals. While this may apply to many in the upper echelons of the organizations that were involved in the crash, it pains me to see the ground rescuers and firemen being painted with the same brush. This was simply owing to the glacial pace of post-crash investigations; PIA's own incompetence had created the idea that everyone who was involved had been lazy or negligent, and the flames of anger burn indiscriminately.

▪

On a personal level as well, this obsession with image building can be toxic. So how can we guard against insincerity when it comes to ourselves? Sincerity necessitates that we mean what we say, but it differs from candour. It does not require the disclosure of everything on your mind, but it does require truthfulness in what you do reveal. According to many philosophers' arguments, then, 'sincerity is perfectly compatible with people keeping secrets, withholding information, or more broadly, being entitled to privacy'.[14]

We are merely ruling out deceiving others, and this deception and untruthfulness is morally objectionable. For consequentialists, this instruction follows from the harmful outcome of untruthful actions. Even if untruthful actions can have positive consequences, most largely agree that they are corrupting in their nature. Deontologists, on the other hand, talk about the inherently bad nature of untruthfulness instead. Deontological discourse is certainly what inspired the more rigid philosophers like Kant.

But these philosophical discussions can often seem far too lofty and idealistic to most of us. Some instances of intentional lies are largely accepted, such as, jokes or white lies, or lies told to protect someone's feelings. Where, then, should we draw the line? Should we hold ourselves to the same standards as we hold politicians' public discourse? Should politicians point to the unrealistic nature of such standards to make their actions seem justifiable?

Even if we do not engage with protracted treatises about the philosophy of sincerity, or think about the long-term repercussions that insincerity can have on global histories, I believe it is imperative for us to examine the beliefs we hold and to think consciously about the lengths we are prepared to go to in order to hold true to our ideals. What degree of sincerity matters to you, in your life and in those around you? What do you expect from your statesmen and your policymakers? When you decide to withhold or expose information, what is the principle underlying the decision that compels your actions? Conscious thought about all of this is far better than making statements in the moment simply because we are pushed by our circumstances. Exploring what matters to you, and what seems inconsequential, gives you a framework for your life, instead of a reactionary approach to the obstacles it throws at you.

I was presented with a fairly convenient opportunity for good press right after my plane crashed. As a nation prone to accepting spiritual explanations for events, people were quick to explain why I had survived the crash. Among the explanations that were floated, one stood out. I had survived, people claimed, because when the rest of the world was flung into turmoil by Covid-19 and businesses began to shut down and lay off workers, I had stuck to my principles and retained my workforce despite the lockdowns, so God had rewarded me for it.

This was patently false—the decision to retain and pay all employees was taken by the board of directors and the previous president of the bank. All I did was stick to it. I made it very clear to employees and friends alike that this decision was not my contribution. At the time, people were hungry for news of the crash, and I did not want to allow this voracious appetite for any kind of feel-good news to eclipse the truth, even if it served my 'image'.

I am not trying to portray myself as the proverbial and dreaded 'good guy' here. I merely want to reiterate that when you have consciously thought about the degree of sincerity with which you want to live your life, and have decided on your principles, actions become much easier, compared to when you are simply going with the flow. I had decided that I valued sincerity above short-term goals. Even if being sincere comes at a cost to me—such as being disliked or losing an advantage in my personal or professional life—I will hold sincerity above the potential positive consequences of untruthfulness.

This is not a lesson I learnt directly from the crash, but I feel it is one that dictates the flow of my life. Tough self-introspection and a candid engagement with complex subjects—whether they relate to your personal lives or societal issues—allows you to predetermine the course of your life and makes you more informed and honest. You may not always like the direction it leads you in, but you will not be driven by baser impulses, and will always value the journey that took you there. More importantly, in the event that you *are* placed in a position of power after a tragedy unfolds, your sincerity may be key to averting a lot of pain.

5

MIRACLES

A Journey Through Survival and Guilt

Yeh zindagi hai sahib
Uljhegi nahin, toh suljhegi kaise?
Bikhregi nahin, toh nikhregi kaise?

This is life, sir.
If it doesn't get complicated, how will it be
simplified?
If it doesn't face disintegration, how will it be
lively again?[1]

I often thought about these lines in the weeks after the crash when I was confined to a hospital bed. I felt as though my body had been wrecked—torn apart completely so it could be reassembled from scratch. I had burnt my back, broken my right arm, and torn the ligaments in my left knee. After several reconstructive surgeries, I had to wait for the other ligaments to grow of their own accord.

Days after I had been admitted, my body continued to find new and inventive ways of reacting to the trauma.

Blood continued to leak from broken capillaries, and I developed haematomas. The doctors needed to remove the necrotic skin and foreign debris that was enmeshed into the healthy skin in my back, and I sat through painful sessions of wound debridement. Two years later, I am still dealing with new medical complications from the battering my body took during the crash.

At the time, I had friends and family to keep me company, but I was wracked with survivor's guilt. For months, I could not bring myself to meet the other survivor or the families of the victims. I struggled to attend funerals without wondering if the family of the deceased resented me—whether my presence would comfort them or be a cruel reminder that I was given a miracle, when their loved ones were not. In the days following the crash, I tried to decipher why I had been spared where so many others had lost their lives.

▪

Miracles are a curious thing. For most of human history they have held people in awe, or bound them to ideas about supernatural forces, myths and gods who would swoop in at the last minute and save them from eternal damnation or certain death. In Graeco-Roman lore, mythological gods like Hercules, Asclepius and Isis regularly performed healing miracles, and even brought people back from the dead. These gods were compelled by their undying compassion for humankind, and its condition in a bleak and often cruel world. The recipients of these miracles, who were cured of plagues or fatal diseases, came from all social ranks and statuses. And so, in a way, miracles were the great equalizer.

Even the death lore of Asclepius—the Roman god of medicine—is a reminder of this. After a centaur (a creature that is supposedly half-human, half-horse) teaches him the art of healing, Asclepius begins to heal the sick in their dreams. This scares the god Zeus into believing that Asclepius' incessant and rapid healing of the sick would eventually make men immortal, so he kills the god of medicine.[2] This myth became so popular that people in ancient Rome began to sleep in Asclepius' temples, hoping for a miraculous reprieve from death.

But stories like these are not limited to the ancient myths. In the Judaeo-Christian-Islamic tradition, miracles abound. It is believed that when Moses was guiding the Israelites out of Egypt, and away from a life of slavery and prosecution, the pursuing forces of the vile pharaoh thundered down the roads behind them on horseback. With a 'sea of reeds' in front of him, and Egyptian soldiers at his back, Moses raised his staff and a strong wind parted the water in the sea, leaving a narrow path across the seabed dry so his believers could walk across it. Once his believers had crossed, the parted sea closed in and made it impossible for their pursuers to follow.[3]

In Christianity, it is believed that Jesus raised the dead. While travelling, he came across a funeral procession in a small village called Nain. The dead man was an only son, whose mother was a widow, so his heart filled with pity.

He told the woman not to weep, and laid his hand on the casket and summoned the boy to rise. The boy woke up and began to talk, and news that a new prophet had arisen travelled quickly over the lands.[4]

Finally, while Muslims believe that Islam's greatest miracle is the Quran, even this religion has its fair share of miraculous tales. In varying versions of this story, Prophet Muhammad is believed to have either cured a blind man by placing his own saliva on the eyelids of the afflicted or cured his cousin Ali ibn Abi Talib of 'eye trouble' by doing the same.[5] While some contest stories like this, they have become a part of the popular narrative within Islam.

It is interesting to note that in almost all these myths and religions, the recipients of these miracles were people who had a faultless moral compass, or people who deserved a break: a downtrodden group of slaves, a widow who could not lose her only son, or a good man with a disability. In all these stories, miracles have one unifying theme. They are proof that the higher powers do not care for social hierarchies, and encourage believers to seek God's favour and divine intervention, by being kind and true and just.

A more modern, cynical observer like Karl Marx would have relegated miracles to a trick in the arsenal of religious dogmas—just one more way for religion to maintain control of the masses, to act as the opiate that kept them calm and resigned to the human condition, and stopped them from rebelling against the status quo.[6]

▪

Before my plane crashed, I had never thought about the nature of miracles. I knew one thing—I had neither the unflinching belief in the power of miracles (that the masses clung to), nor the disdain for miracles that non-religious folk exhibited. Put simply, I did not have the time or the inclination to hope for a miracle to improve my condition.

I suppose this was a function of my privilege. I had grown up in a family that, despite belonging squarely in the middle class, was well educated and open-minded. We had exposure to the world, and we luckily avoided the sort of extreme circumstances (like poverty) that force the fervent wish for and reliance on miracles.

Because I had been raised as a Muslim, I did not necessarily contradict the existence of miracles, but I did not feel like I needed an inexplicable, miraculous event to help me climb the social ladder. Like my family, I clung to a belief in diligent, tireless work, and in meritocracy—not just at the level of professional engagement or employment, but also on a deeper philosophical level.

After the crash, confined to a hospital bed—dealing with the torturous wanderings of a mind that does not understand why something has happened—it took a while for me to realize how much of the popular narratives about miracles I had subconsciously internalized. I fell into the trap of thinking that I should have done something to deserve this survival because otherwise it made no sense.

Was it down to some good that I had done? I racked my brains and made a moral inventory. I could say that

I had always valued sincerity, integrity and hard work, and had always unflinchingly told the truth, even when it went against my own interests. But this was something my parents, and my extended family and friends, had drilled in me. So my moral compass (for better or worse) was a product of my parents' upbringing. Why, then, had I been saved?

I realized then how flawed I was in internalizing the popular narratives surrounding miracles and thinking that I had done anything to deserve one. I could not come to terms with a world in which people who must have been kinder, or more hard-working, or more generous, or simply younger (and still uncorrupted by the vagaries of time) had died and I had lived. I felt guilty and to appease this guilt, I wondered whether I was worthy of this reprieve from death.

The truth is that I was saved for no apparent reason, other than my parents' prayers. I am eternally grateful that they were not forced to weather the most tumultuous storm of them all—the loss of a child. I know that being wracked by such insurmountable grief was unthinkable for them, and I am forever in awe of the grave resilience and grace displayed by the parents who lost their children in this crash.

My being alive was truly a miracle, but it was one I could not question. According to the European Transport Safety Council, 90 per cent of aircraft accidents are technically survivable.[7] If the plane's structure remains intact, the impact is tolerable for its occupants, and the post-crash environment does not pose a threat to the rescuers, then people survive. In our case, all three of these conditions were overturned. In the short but celebrated history of aviation, you will not find many survivors of planes that crashed and were subsequently engulfed in flames. My life, then, had simply been saved because of a series of fortunate events.

▪

I was long notorious for arriving late at airports, and even my early arrival was out of character. In 2010, I was returning to Pakistan after a stint as the regional managing director and CEO of Barclays in southern Africa (in Zambia) for slightly over two years. I was responsible for managing the southern Africa region (comprising Zambia, Botswana and Zimbabwe) and the bank grew significantly during my tenure, with 10,000 people and US$3 billion in assets. The three franchises were the largest and the oldest in their respective jurisdictions, so the high-profile nature of this job meant that I had become quite well known within the Pakistani diaspora and otherwise in Zambia—a country of 12 million people. In any case, nothing unites Pakistanis like living in a foreign country. The romanticized collective memory of home forges indescribably strong bonds, so my permanent relocation had been endlessly discussed and a great sense of melancholy pervaded the interactions I had before leaving.

I adored my friends in Africa, but I am not one for melodrama. To avoid drawn-out farewells at home and at the airport (where another crowd of Pakistanis had gathered to see me off), I had left my house much earlier than I usually did.

At the check-in counter, a beautiful African lady greeted me. She took one look at my travel documents, and confusing me for one of the protocol officers who usually arrived at the airport before me asked where Mr Zafar Masud was. 'That's me,' I said with a grin. 'Stand up, everyone! Stand up and clap for this gentleman,' she said, addressing the room. A few people looked at her warily, while others mustered a half-hearted spatter of applause.

I had not caught on. I was still riding high on the outpouring of love the Pakistani community had showered upon me, so I assumed that this greeting was for a job well done at the country's largest bank. 'You have given us so much trouble for over two years,' she said with a smirk. 'Our officials have to look for you all over the airport before your plane takes off. But you're finally on time!' I was mortified, but my flying habits did not really change in the years that followed or even now, a fact which I am not particularly proud of. Suffice to say, then, that my early arrival at the airport on the day of the crash was in itself an aberration of the highest order. It may have saved my life.

As mentioned previously, upon arriving early, I realized that my new protocol officer had got me a window seat, but upon request, I was allotted Seat 1C, on the aisle side of the very front row, which was crucial to my survival. If this seat had not been ejected when the plane's hull cracked open, I would have remained trapped inside when the plane went up in flames. The way in which I was then saved and removed from the area also beggars belief. The location of my seat, the physics of my fall, the kindness of strangers in the street—all conspired to keep me alive. In the early days after the crash, I struggled with this. I had post-traumatic stress, and I was only saved from agonizing flashbacks because I had lost consciousness during the most horrific part of the ordeal.

Unlike Zubair, I was neither responsible for rescuing myself, nor even conscious for most of it. My survival was purely a miracle: nothing more and nothing less. As a result, I did not have to relive such painful memories. I had only God to thank.

However, for days I was clearly grappling with the guilt of having survived, and this was manifesting itself in the frenzied search for meaning that I had embarked on. To reiterate, I don't know why I was saved. I don't know why I was given a miracle. It was only when I made peace with not knowing that I was able to move on. The constant support I received from friends, family and strangers helped me immensely. In some instances, this outpouring of love was directed at me simply because people were desperate to cling to any kind of good news that they could salvage from an otherwise horrible tragedy, but it humbled me beyond measure.

What I have learnt is that I can only look to the future. My faith in miracles, in the baffling, inexplicable will of God, has been reinforced, but it is not something I can dwell on. What is in my control, and in yours, is how we live what remains of our lives.

With fellow members of the board of directors of the Oil & Gas Development Company Limited in 2024

With fellow members of the board of directors of the Bank of Punjab (BOP) in 2023

Recognized for my work by my previous employer in 2023

Recognized for my work by my alma mater in 2023

Honoured to be the chief guest at the graduation ceremony of the National University of Sciences & Technology in 2023

Receiving the fourth highest state order of Hungary for supporting the restoration of August Schoefft's 175-year-old paintings from the Princess Bamba Collection in 2021

My first appearance in a cartoon, including caricatures of the BOP head office and a Pakistan International Airlines plane, in one of the local publications after the crash

My second appearance in a cartoon, appreciating my work related to government-sponsored schemes for the benefit of common citizens, in one of the local publications

EULOGY PK8303 CRASH ANNIVERSARY

One year on, the single biggest facet that keeps me traumatized about the crash is the fact that this entire fateful ordeal resulted in the loss of 97 innocent lives. 22nd May 2020 was one of the saddest days in our lives and will remain so forever.

God has been very kind on me and I have been managing my recovery well, including psychiatric counseling, medical treatment, etc., with the unwavering support of my employer & colleagues, and my family & friends. I am extremely thankful for the prayers of all known and unknown well wishers during the past one year.

However, as I worked towards my recuperation, particularly mental, let me share with you that I discovered other complications of sufferings. I realized that I have been immersed with "survivor's guilt". I could not bring myself to meet with the other survivor or the families of victims. I struggled to attend funerals without thinking that the family of the deceased must be wondering why I was given a miracle, when their loved ones were not. This is probably the most difficult phase of my life which I am still struggling to get over with great deal of endeavor.

Unfortunately, even after the lapse of 12-months of this crash, which was the 6th Pakistani plane to crash in a decade, nothing soberly changed at the national level to improve passenger safety. I believe that we at least need to bring domestic flight standards at par with international ones, and enforce standardized procedures to handle crashes and their aftermath. I believe that the entire echo-system needs to be reviewed and revamped to ensure better safety and security standards.

This is why I have decided to set-up a not-for-profit organization which would be dedicated to work on passenger safety and security. The foundation will have two main functions - firstly, work on raising awareness about passenger safety and their rights within the civil society; and secondly, work with policy makers to improve standards & regulations, push for legislative change & their implementation, and ensuring better legal assistance & coverage for affectees.

On the first anniversary of this tragic incident, may God rest the departed souls in peace and give strength to their families to bear their irreparable loss. Aameen!

ZAFAR MASUD
21ˢᵗ May 2021 (Lahore, Pakistan)

My eulogy on the first anniversary of the crash on 21 May 2021

My first television appearance after the crash on a popular Urdu talk show in 2021, which was widely watched and appreciated

My first interview after the crash, which was published in a business magazine in 2020

Immensely proud of travelling via the same airline—on the same seat, and on the same flight—to overcome my fear of flying in late 2020

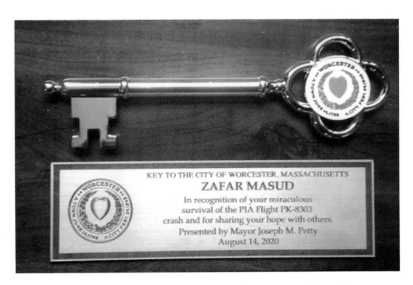

Honoured to be recognized by the Mayor of Worcester, Massachusetts, on Pakistan National Day in Boston in 2020

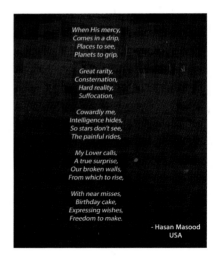

Date: 22nd Sept 20.

وصل کی اک شام

(handwritten Urdu poem)

When His mercy,
Comes in a drip,
Places to see,
Planets to grip,

Great rarity,
Consternation,
Hard reality,
Suffocation,

Cowardly me,
Intelligence hides,
So stars don't see,
The painful rides,

My Lover calls,
A true surprise,
Our broken walls,
From which to rise,

With near misses,
Birthday cake,
Expressing wishes,
Freedom to make.

— Hasan Masood
USA

A poem written in Urdu after my crash by an admirer who wants to remain anonymous

A poem written by my cousin, Hasan Masood, after the crash

MIRACLE ON A MODEL COLONY STREET

Andrea Corr, the lead singer of my favourite band 'The Corrs', sent me a video message, wishing a speedy recovery, and a signed copy of her memoir—courtesy of my dear Irish friend, Maria-Pia Kelly. 'Borrowed Heaven' by The Corrs kept me going after the crash; each and every word of the song resonates perfectly with me

An op-ed by my dear niece, Nida Zehra, after the crash, published in *Dawn* on 7 June 2020

Zafar Masud
President & CEO

May 24, 2020

Dear Colleagues

As you all are aware that flight PK-8303 of Pakistan International Airline (PIA) crashed in Karachi on Friday just before landing and I was also onboard of this unfortunate plane. This was indeed a horrific incident which resulted in loss of around 97 precious lives including passengers and aircrew. By the Grace of Allah Swt, I was among the only two survivors of plane crash. Considering the devastation caused by the crash, miraculously, I have sustained only a few injuries and being taken good care of by the medical team. Alhamdulillah, I am feeling much better now.

Reliving the ordeal of ill-fated plane, I found myself very lucky to survive against all odds. I strongly believe that this was all due to the prayers of my family, friends and specially thousands of members of BOP family.

I express my deepest condolences on behalf of The Bank of Punjab to families of passengers and aircrew members who have lost their lives. I pray to Allah to grant them highest ranks in eternal life and also give solace to bereaved families.

I am very proud of all staff members of my BOP team and grateful for their prayers & best wishes. I also feel proud that I am heading an institution where everyone cares about each other. In Sha Allah very soon I will be among you and together we will work for the progress and prosperity of the Bank. This incident has further strengthen my resolve to work with more zeal and fervor for the welfare of all of you. It is high time to make a pledge to continue caring about each other and work for the growth of our Bank.

I believe that Allah Swt has given me a second life and I wish to make the most of it by serving my Country, this Institution and working for the betterment of all of you.

Eid Mubarak to all of you and your families.

Warm Regards

Zafar Masud
President/CEO

President Secretariat - Head Office: BOP Tower, 10-B, Block E/II, Main Boulevard, Gulberg III, Lahore.
Ph. Office: +92 (42) 35783711-12, Fax: +92 (42) 35783713 Web: www.bop.com.pk, e-mail: zafar.masud@bop.com.pk

www.bop.com.pk   UAN: 111 200 100

My communication with my colleagues after the crash on 24 May 2020

News broadcast about my survival a few hours after the crash

Wreckage of the unlucky flight

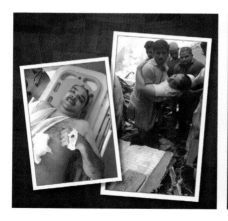

My urgent rescue reinforced my faith in humanity

My boarding pass stub from the ill-fated flight

With fellow board members of the National Bank of Pakistan in 2019

With fellow board members of the State Bank of Pakistan in 2013

With the first president of Zambia, Kenneth Kaunda, in 2009

With fellow members of the board of directors of the southern Africa region of Barclays, Zambia, in 2008

Starting my professional journey with the American Express Bank, Karachi, in 1993

With my entire family, who are my strength, my heart and my soul

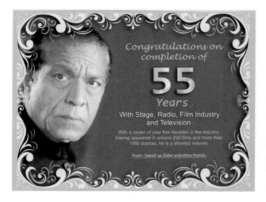

Exceptionally proud of my father, Munawar Saeed—my idol and my inspiration—for having completed 55 years in the film and television industry

My father in the all-time super-hit television drama serial *Waris* in 1979

My father's first appearance on the silver screen in *Ghar Damaad* in 1969

My parents with the maternal side of the family

With my siblings in 1987

Ready to take on the world at the tender age of five in 1975

With my grandparents on my first birthday in 1971

All decked up for my first birthday in 1971

As a newborn with my parents in 1970

My parents with friends and family after their wedding in 1969

My father with the paternal side of the family in Amroha in 1952

6

WILLPOWER

Overcoming Trauma and Reclaiming Life

The crash itself was harrowing, but it was a blip in time. For me, the real struggle began in the hospital bed. This journey was cumbersome and painful. The mind, once the body is harmed in the way mine was, requires unflagging determination to soldier on through physical pain in pursuit of a long-term goal. It was through sheer willpower that I forced my way through that agony, and began working from the hospital bed a month after the crash.

Ironically, it had begun as a seemingly tame affair. We initially thought that my injuries were fairly straightforward. One of my hands was broken and my back was burnt. One of my knees hurt incessantly, but I assumed these were all easily fixable issues. A friend of mine even told me that it seemed as though I had fallen from a bicycle instead of a plane.

It was not until a week later, when the doctors finally did an MRI of the knee in question, that we realized how badly it had been damaged. I had lost ligaments which would have to be replaced, and had breaks in my bones that would need grafting. A second surgery was planned and carried out, in which a piece of bone from my pelvis was grafted on to my arm. As for the ligaments in my legs, the doctors tried to salvage one that was partially broken. In simple terms, it was tied with a string and left to heal on its own. This did not work out in the long run, and years later, I had to seek treatment abroad.

The slow realization that my injuries were much more extensive and life-altering than they initially appeared was devastating. But while I had to draw on reserves of willpower I never previously thought I had, this helped me regain some semblance of normalcy in my life, which hastened my recovery. I realized that life and meaningful work are inseparable. In fact, the latter may even provide the impetus for a life well lived—especially if you are fortunate enough to love your work, which is true in my case. But even for those of you who sometimes deal with a little drudgery or monotony in your workplaces, work and its associated distractions can, at times, be a lifesaver. I certainly needed the work I was doing in order to recover from the trauma, and in return my persistence allowed a bank of national significance to continue to thrive.

I still believe that one of the reasons why I recovered so quickly from this psychological trauma was this iron-willed tenacity and drive to continue to work. I could not have relied entirely on my own faculties, frayed and vulnerable as they were, for this recovery. I had to do everything in my power to fuel this will, and that road was not easy.

■

Physically, my body is still recovering from the injuries it sustained. Immediately after the crash, I went through four operations: two on my arm, one on my knee, and one on my back. My leg presented the most problems. I had lost two ligaments completely and a third was torn. The doctors in Karachi were clear that they lacked the necessary resources to address the issues in my leg, but my passport (with all its visa stamps) got lost in the crash, so we had to wait. The rest of my body recovered, and my doctors in Pakistan came up with the makeshift arrangement for my leg, in which the partially damaged ligament was held together with a string and prayers. This was not ideal, but it was the best they could offer with the technology available to them. It would require six months for the swelling in my body to go down before I could seek a more permanent solution for the torn ligaments.

Between this makeshift solution, the trappings of international travel after the pandemic, and Pakistan's placement on the red list, I ended up struggling for almost a year and a half before I was first able to fly to London. Either this year or later, I expect to go for another treatment, that of bone grafting, to further strengthen this leg, and I may require a complete knee replacement for full recovery. And I have just recently discovered that I also have issues in my spinal cord, treatment for which may be required either immediately or within the next decade but until then, I will have to resort on aid to walk, which keeps reminding me about the trauma I had experienced. I guess that's life and I have to live with it that way only.

The days that led up to the surgery on my leg were difficult for me. The mind is a curious thing: it can hold two contrary opinions at once. I was grateful for my survival in the most absurd circumstances, and I understood that I had been luckier than all passengers (barring one other) on that plane, so I could not complain. But as weeks of recovery turned into months, the pain and isolation began to weigh on me. I had to cling to the remaining shreds of willpower that I had developed during my first stint at the hospital to get through this time.

My mobility was extremely limited. I could not sit for too long, or bend my knee because of the wire bracing it. My office was accessible, so I could at least continue to work, but my social life was now severely limited. Hanging out with friends, which had previously been a lifeline for me, was no longer easy, and neither was attending the important (and sometimes high-profile) events I needed to attend for work. This isolation sometimes hung heavier than the injuries I had sustained.

At other times, the pain from the lateral injury on my leg took centre stage. The nerves are crucial to complete recovery. Mine were substantially compressed. For a year and a half, I was at a risk of getting a blood clot in my head if the nerve became completely choked. This obviously would have created far greater problems than the ones I had initially anticipated.

In November 2021, an excruciating year and a half after the plane crash, I finally flew out to London for the surgery I needed. I recognize that I am privileged in being able to afford such a procedure in the first place. The damages paid by the airline would not have even covered a fraction of the cost of my surgeries.

The doctors assessed my knees and concluded that the right knee did not look too bad. At worst, it felt weak and achy. The doctors considered a platelet-rich plasma (PRP) injection therapy. Put simply, they would inject my own platelets into the area to accelerate the healing, and to address any musculoskeletal problems there.

The left knee, however, was a mess. I had a nerve injury that affected both branches of the sciatic nerve. The damage to the common peroneal nerve made my great toe slightly weak. It needed to be carefully dissected in a procedure known as neurolysis. The damage to the tibial nerve changed the sensation in my shin. If this was further damaged during surgery, I would be at risk of permanent weakness in the foot.

My surgeons planned on taking out the wires embedded in my leg—drilling a tunnel through the fibula head to reconstruct the lateral ligament—and doing a separate reconstruction of the popliteus. To fix the anterior cruciate ligament, I was to receive a donated graft of human tissue. For the posterior, the surgeons intended to use a synthetic graft.[1]

I had the best surgeons I could have hoped for, but I still ran the risk of infection. If the site of the surgery did in fact become infected, I would have to undergo yet another procedure to wash the infection away, or even have to get all of the hardware removed and inserted again. There was also the risk of blood clots, which my surgeons wanted to minimize with anticoagulants. And finally, there was a risk from anaesthesia, although minimal. Perhaps the biggest risk was stiffness after surgery. The hope was that this would be addressed through physiotherapy, but it could require further surgery if it persisted.

I was dealing with doctors who were required to divulge as much information as possible by law. Suddenly, I understood why some Pakistani doctors often gave bewilderingly hazy explanations of their procedures—not knowing the details certainly keeps patients in good spirits. But here, I had a very clear picture of the surgery and the risks associated with it, and I was frightened by them. A few days before the surgery, as the doctor listed them one by one, I almost backed out. I understood the need for informed consent, but I almost wished for a return to the 19th-century practice of keeping patients completely oblivious to any potential risks that could be upsetting. I had to be reassured that my chances were good, before I gave consent.

And so, on the day of the surgery, my doctors meant to perform multiple procedures while I was under anaesthesia. First, a keyhole surgery to diagnose the problems, then a removal of the hardware already embedded in my leg, then a neurolysis of the common peroneal nerve, reconstructions of the anterior and posterior cruciate ligaments, and finally an injection of PRP.

When the surgeons cut into my leg, they noticed that the common peroneal nerve was 50 per cent stenosed (or compressed). It was surrounded by dense adhesions that had to be excised. Having freed the nerve up, they proceeded towards the reconstruction. The first drill hole converged with the nerve tunnels, so they drilled a second hole for the ligament reconstruction. Beyond that, the surgery proceeded as intended. At the end of the procedure, there was a full range of motion, no impingement and excellent stability.[2]

This did not mean that I could run laps in a park. I still had weeks of physiotherapy left, with precise instructions on how much load I could bear during these sessions. The doctors wanted me to go for full movement, and to avoid wearing a brace to bed. When I was up and about, I wore a TROM (total range of motion) brace for around four weeks. Even now, I must wear another big brace if I intend to walk a small distance.

At that time, other than an hour every day, I was largely confined to a bed. Walking to a restaurant 20 minutes away from the apartment I was renting in London was a struggle, and it sapped the dregs of energy I had left. I had to stop twice on the way, and wait for the pain and stiffness to subside before moving. It would take a year for me to fully recover after the surgery.

I have never craved normalcy more than I did in those days. Knowing that you are impaired or compromised in some way erects a mental block unlike any other. The physical blocks were problematic enough; once again, I could not sit for too long in meetings or socialize. This time, I didn't even have a lot of family and friends nearby to help with the recuperation on a daily basis. The few family members who were nearby were all extremely helpful, and I am deeply grateful to them for their help.

On the one hand, I had a renewed vigour for life, courtesy of my survival in the crash. On the other, physical injuries and isolation continued to test this vigour. I also felt pangs of survivor's guilt—not just for surviving, but also for letting treatable medical issues dampen my spirit. I had to come to terms with the fact that while my problems were trivial in comparison to the lives lost, they still deserved time, attention and care. As someone who had vowed to live my life as an agent of change for the community at large, this acknowledgement felt self-indulgent (even selfish) but it was necessary for my emotional recovery.

In addition to what was immediately obvious to the doctors, the crash continued to spin out new and confounding complications for my body. Two years later, I found out that there had been a significant shift in my spinal cord, reversing the alignment of the L4/L5 vertebrae, and I began to experience blinding pain. It became impossible to stand straight or walk around alone.

Slowly, I have learnt to get used to the barrage of medical information that is thrown my way whenever a new issue arises. Despite having no inclination to do so, I find myself being introduced to new disciplines in medical science. After two years of daily physiotherapy, I am now familiarizing myself with osteopathy—something I had not even heard of before.

All of this means that I still have to use a wheelchair at airports and in places where long walks are warranted. For the next year or two, the situation is not expected to change. I was not a young man before the crash, but I had no medical issues and enjoyed considerably good health and energy. Nothing could have prepared me for the frustration that would come with the loss of being an able-bodied individual, and the constant revision of my own expectations about what I could physically do.

I still have issues that require attention—the doctors must replace my knee, perform an osteotomy, and fix the ligaments that still need fixing. This can be done in one long complex operation, or split into three smaller surgeries. This is something my medical team will embark on if and when my knee gives in completely. Until then, I must try to retain a sense of normalcy and draw on the strength I have developed in order to continue as usual.

▪

Dealing with a mental disconnect with the body I find myself in, and having to perform and deliver at a fast-paced job without using my physical constraints as an impediment or a crutch is a noble pursuit. However, in the daily struggle of routine, it is not a pursuit I would romanticize. The truth is that the struggle was brutal, and while a strong will allows you to face impossible situations, the struggle remains ugly and brutal for many people—especially those with chronic disabilities. And our world remains inaccessible for many.

Bizarrely, these epiphanies helped me grow emotionally, until I was perhaps stronger than I felt before the crash. I found out recently that I was not the only person to have experienced such improvement. In a study presented at the 107th annual convention of the American Psychological Association in Boston in 1999, the researchers had examined the long-term effects of trauma on plane crash survivors, and found that they may be better off than travellers who fly frequently but had never been in a crash. Although the sample size was small (15 plane crash survivors and 8 people who had never been in a crash), the results were striking.[3]

They found that the 'psychological well-being of airplane crash survivors compared to air travellers who have never been involved in any type of aviation accident or crash was much better on all the levels measured. The crash survivors actually scored lower on several standardized measures of emotional distress than the flyers who hadn't been in an accident.'[4]

This is not to suggest that crashes are good, but perhaps it points to the human brain's resilience when faced with wanton destruction and trauma—it shows us a glimmer of what we can achieve when we set our mind to it. Sometimes, it just takes a devastating incident to trigger that reliance on your will and that renewed dedication to living a better life. Some of the earliest men and women who tested their wills in feats of endurance are proof of this.

In 490 BC, two of the greatest civilizations of their time, the Greek and the Persians, clashed on the plain of Marathon in Greece, just off the Petalioi Gulf.[5] For Greece, the threat loomed large. The Persian army was around three times the size of the Greek troops, and was trained in deadly combat. Athenian generals were so demoralized by the incoming army that they almost chose not to fight. But after a close vote, they galvanized their forces and ushered them to Marathon to take a stand.

While I am compelled to mention these armies and the battle they fought, this is not their story. I merely mention them to bring up Pheidippides,[6] a humble messenger in the employ of the Greek forces. You see, while the Greeks showed remarkable resolve in their willingness to fight rather than surrender, they also understood that they were greatly outnumbered. They needed more troops, and so they sought help from Sparta—known for producing the most formidable fighters in their corner of the world.

Sparta lay a full 150 miles from Marathon, and the Greeks needed to send a messenger who was fast and physically fit. The Greek general Miltiades chose Pheidippides to carry the plea to the distant city. He, in turn, ran for *two days* to get to Sparta before the Persians arrived. He then ran all the way back to Miltiades, carrying the news of their refusal to help and allowing the general to plan accordingly.

Meanwhile, the Persians made a grievous error. While Greek forces gathered in Marathon, Athens lay undefended. Seeking to take advantage of this and avoid a drawn-out battle that would incur casualties on both sides, the Persian army tried to sail towards Athens in the middle of the night, leaving a retinue of soldiers to keep the Greeks engaged in Marathon. But the Greeks were on home ground. When they saw how evenly matched the Persian army remaining in Marathon was, they attacked and nearly obliterated the Persians who were left behind. In just three hours, the Persians suffered incalculable losses and were forced to retreat back to the remaining ships.

Meanwhile, Miltiades sent ahead Pheidippides to Athens to warn them that a large portion of the Persian fleet had broken off and intended to attack the city, and also to marshal them with news of Greece's victory in Marathon. Once again, Pheidippides ran for an astounding 25 miles to deliver the message.

By this time, his body barely held together. It is common knowledge that people engaging in long-distance running experience shortness of breath, extreme discomfort in the upper body, chest pains and light-headedness. His feet must already have developed bunions, the unsightly protrusions that modern runners dread. Perhaps they even bled. His muscles must have ached with every step, pains must have shot through his body with every advance. But while we know little of Pheidippides' life and motivations, we know that he had an indefatigable will and he was determined to reach the city before the Persian fleet.

He managed to do just that, shouting, 'Rejoice! We have victory!' before he collapsed and died where he had fallen. There was a huge uproar—the city cheered and then awaited the return of troops over land with bated breath. Despite the Persian ships having a head start, Miltiades and his men marched in full armour back to Athens and arrived before the Persians. When the Persians finally neared Athens and saw the battle-weary Greeks already in place—still ready to fight after defeating part of their army in Marathon—they were so demoralized that they returned to Persia. The battle allowed Greek cities to develop and prosper for years without Persian interference.

I marvel at the will of not just the soldiers defending the Greek cities but also the messengers who ran until their bodies gave out. Pheidippides' story has so enthralled successive generations that when the Olympic games were finally reinstated in 1896, a long-distance race was introduced. It was to be called a 'marathon'. In the years since, marathon runners have trained themselves to run ever more gruelling distances in all kinds of weather. The stress and fatigue of the endeavour has the potential to send runners into cardiac arrest (which is most likely what happened to Pheidippides) but they soldier on through harder and harder challenges.

I do not think I understood how much regard I had for

this iron will until I was forced on the slow march towards physical recovery after the plane crash. Many centuries later, the experiences of endurance athletes are just as inspiring as that of Pheidippides. Much like him, these athletes run extraordinary distances during their races. Take Courtney Dauwalter, an ultramarathon runner who was featured in *The New York Times* for 'outrunning the men'.[7] Ultramarathons can cover distances of 200 miles or more; one such race, nicknamed Big's Backyard Ultra, requires participants to complete a 4.16-mile loop every hour. If they need to eat or go to the bathroom, they have to run faster to make up for the time. The last man or woman standing wins. Dauwalter ran for 67 hours before conceding to the victor. In many races, she has left male ultrarunners behind and gone on to nab the title.

According to the article, as the distance increases, the physical advantages that men have over women become more and more insignificant. The race becomes about stamina; something dependent on a combination of strength and willpower. Some experts quoted in the article, such as Heather Heying, are not surprised by this. Perhaps women's long evolutionary history of giving birth and enduring pain gives them a stronger will or a psychological edge in endurance events. However, some others are not convinced.[8]

But Dauwalter certainly runs far longer than someone who has not put themselves through endurance training. Sometimes, while she runs, she is hallucinating live puppets playing on a swing set or trees and rocks that turned into faces. Whether or not there is enough data to conclusively prove if an iron will can eclipse physical or biological advantages, ultramarathoners are certainly a testament to the will of both male and female runners, sharpened to a point where running for 40 or even 60 hours becomes a possibility.

I do not adhere to the point of view that *all* issues can be overcome with a strong will—that kind of approach stems from able-bodied privilege. Unfortunately, it also places blame on those who suffer from permanent disabilities of any form. Goodness of character or strength of will does not cure anyone. In many instances, physical recovery is not possible.

But wherever it is possible, it is evident that developing your willpower, learning to delay instant gratification for long-term goals, and powering through short-term pain and pressure can work wonders.

This applies to all of our struggles. We may not be interested in testing the limits of our physical endurance by running long distances, but we all have struggles: skills we want to develop, habits we wish to drop, obstacles we need to overcome. Unfortunately, many of us firmly believe we do not belong in the same league as people like Dauwalter, or that their unflagging resolve is of mythic proportions—inspirational but unattainable. It is a defeatist and pessimistic assumption, but one that many of us make as though it is obvious.

It should not take a major injury or obstacle for us to test our mettle and show us what we can achieve if we put our minds to it. Simple, conscious efforts, such as practising cognitive reframing when met with seemingly insurmountable tasks can help. Multiple behavioural therapists expound the benefits of reframing.[9] They report that even recognizing and stopping burdensome thoughts such as 'I should' or 'I ought to', and consciously replacing them with alternatives like 'I will' or 'I choose to' does wonders for people who are struggling.[10]

Unfortunately, we have become so used to defeatist assumptions about ourselves that we often scoff at the idea of mental practices like this. But we owe it to ourselves to try and be kind to ourselves, to be our own advocates, and to change our perception of what we think we can do. Whether we achieve this by engaging in therapy, meditating, or actively defining our goals and working towards them, it is an effort we owe ourselves. By doing so, you can test the very limits of what you thought was possible, perform inhuman feats, and recover from devastating emotional damage. Your will can move mountains!

7

RITUALS

Embracing the Power and Pitfalls of Tradition

The circumstances of my crash and my excruciatingly slow recovery—which is still under way five years later, and is likely to take another few years if no new hidden injuries crop up—meant that I was forced to immediately acknowledge some of the lessons I am writing about.

A few of these lessons had all the subtlety of a Freightliner making its way down a narrow road. Arrogance was rife in the system; my survival was a miracle. I did not have to struggle to understand any of this. The conclusion was immediate and obvious, almost as if the lesson was thrust upon me with the cataclysmic force of the collision.

But there were also lessons I learnt that were slow to seep in, lessons that revealed themselves during the days I was confined to my hospital bed (or even much later).

These came to me as I replayed what had happened to
me on a continuous loop in my brain—marvelling at the
implausibility of my survival or dissecting the sequence of
events with the exactitude of a clockmaker designing the
precision mechanical apparatus of an antique watch.

Tick.

*I take an abrasive stone and try to sharpen the edges
of my memory, chiselling away at the fog forming into
something dense and concrete, like rust that erodes the
time I spent wading in and out of consciousness.*

Tick.

*I wield that memory like a tool, but I must put it through
another lathe operation, turning away everything that is
irrelevant so I can compare it to the news reports and
unofficial leaks that I encounter.*

Tick.

*I pick them apart with every tool at my disposal. I
construct a timeline, placing the smallest snippets of
relevant developments in their proper place, just like
a clockmaker painstakingly places the tiniest cogs into
place. I get as close to a coherent narrative as I can.*

Boom.

Perhaps my dissection and exactitude were not as cold or
impersonal as a clockmaker's may be. But in the months

following the crash, I certainly felt like I was on par with the aforementioned artisans in the rigorous and repetitive search for order. This vivisection was almost like a ritual, one that helped me make sense of the world post the crash.

It was only later, when I reflected on this, that I discovered the research on the anxiolytic effects of rituals and began to think about how rituals have shaped humans, perhaps since the beginning of salient thought. This naturally led me to question how much focus we should place on rituals in our lives.

▪

It is interesting to note what literature says about rituals. Researchers have often claimed that rituals have psychological benefits for their practitioners.[1] They are ubiquitous across the span of recorded history, and can take a variety of shapes. Sometimes they are performed in communal settings, and at other times in the spiritual comfort of solitude. Some ease mourning and others display collective joy. Some are repetitive and involve physical motions, while others are meditative, silent, singular.

What is interesting to note is that researchers claim that rituals can help with their intended objective. In one of the earliest studies exploring the relationship between rituals and anxiety, anthropologist Bronisław Malinowski studied Melanesian islanders in the early 1900s. He found that Trobriand fishermen engaged in rituals when they expected difficulties. In the rough, tempestuous regions where sharks circled, the fishermen performed elaborate rituals for safety and protection. In calmer waters, they did not perform any rituals. He concluded that whenever an outcome was beyond human control and important, rituals helped to alleviate stress and anxiety.[2] One can theorize that this also helped improve performance.

Some anthropologists have argued that this reduction in anxiety comes about because of the cognitive mechanisms involved while engaging in a ritualistic behaviour. They argue that threats such as 'predation, intrusion by strangers, contamination, contagion, social offence, and harm to offspring' activate mental security systems. In an effort to avoid or stave off these threats, humans often engage in repetitive, scripted actions. The focus on these acts takes up working memory, shifting the focus from the concerning issue to the act being performed.[3]

To understand this, consider the following scenario: 'You live in a small village. Your house is 20 paces from the village well and it is your only source of water. One night, you wake up to the smell of acrid smoke. You realize that your house is on fire. You quickly evacuate your family and your most treasured belongings, and run to the well with a bucket. Meanwhile, the fire is fuelled by a low wind. It creeps up to the rafters of your house, engulfing one side completely.

You haul 20 litres of water up the old well, pour it into your bucket, run 20 paces to your house and try to douse the fire by throwing the entire bucket of water on to the flames. The flames seem to retreat a little. Others join you.

You run back to the well, haul up another bucket, pour it into yours, run back to your house and hurl the water on the flames again. Your muscles strain under the pressure, your heart rate rises and a faint sheen of sweat begins to cover your brow. You run back to the well again, and again, and again, until the motion becomes second nature, in the hope of saving what remains.

According to some researchers, performing the constant, repetitive motion described above would dominate your brain.[4] It would push terror and desperation and anxiety over potentially losing your house to a corner, until the repetitive motion swallows all thought and consumes all your energy. It would lower your anxiety by forcing you to think only about your next step.

More recently, quantitative studies have tried to replicate the results of Malinowski's observations. In one study, golfers with fixed pre-performance routines showcased improved attention and confidence.[5] In another, performing ablutions in a local temple reduced the anxiety participants reported feeling after they were asked to engage in stressful activities like public speaking.[6]

However, this effect has varied across studies. In one paper, Johannes Alfons Karl and Ronald Fischer reported performing a competitive test of the benefits of rituals for stress. His contention was that rituals 'reduce existential anxiety and uncertainty', and he tested this by recreating two underlying mechanisms of rituals: cognitive load and repetitive movement.[7] Karl failed to find support for the idea that rituals have such a large cognitive load that they could crowd out anxiety. Nevertheless, he did find that increasing stress led to participants performing more repetitive behaviour, which in turn reduced the physiological signs of stress.

Despite variations, all of these studies have had some significant results, and they perhaps explain the crux of ritualistic behaviour. If repetitive, obsessive, rigid behaviour helps reduce anxiety in deadly situations, is it still beneficial to perform such behaviour even when it is not tied to direct outcomes such as the dousing of a fire? Does repeating a prayer to your god have a similar calming effect because of the existence of the deity or because of the repetition itself? And is this why rituals have permeated cultures across different times and places?

It bears mentioning that the scenario outlined above involved a ritual that was devised for the task at hand, that is, it had no emotional link to the participants' belief systems. Rituals performed for religious or social reasons may have the added placebo effect that faith can trigger.

▪

Religious and social groups often use rituals to create and preserve their collective identities, according to Joseph Hermanowicz and Harriet Morgan.[8] Saroglou contends that major religions bond their members through ritual practices,[9] while Qiao Wu explains that ritual 'functions as visualization and activation' of an ethnic group's exclusive cultural facts.[10]

Think of the Hajj, the pilgrimage that many Muslims make to Mecca, Saudi Arabia, once a year. The Hajj is defined by a strict adherence to multiple ritual practices, from the ways in which the body is cleansed to the clothes that the Hajjis don, or the number of times the *kaaba* (the house of God) is encircled. Everything is defined with an exacting precision, and this functions both as a highly personal, transcendent, spiritual experience and also as an overt display of one's faith—an act committed with thousands of other Muslims in a place that fosters feelings of brotherhood and community.

The Hajj is a 1,400-year-old ritual. Even more recent rituals, triggered by openings made as a result of geopolitical developments, have quickly taken hold in certain communities within Muslims. The Arbaeen, a pilgrimage to the revered Imam Hussain's shrine, became one of the largest processions of Shia Muslims after the fall of Saddam Hussein's government post 9/11. In an area that was previously hostile to minority faiths, Shia Muslims suddenly had the freedom to openly mourn as they would. In a matter of years, the number of pilgrims for the Arbaeen rose dramatically. In 2024, more than 21 million people made the pilgrimage, eclipsing other religious pilgrimages.[11] Volunteers showed up to provide free food, water and shelter to all who made the journey, and governments began to find ways to cater to the influx. Thus, the Arbaeen became a triumphant declaration of the Shia identity, even though the sentiments that fuelled this ritual were grief and a sense of loyalty to the imams.

The same principle does apply to all collective rituals, whether they are the Hindu celebration of Holi or the anointing of the sick in Catholicism. Ultimately, then, rituals help alleviate individual anxieties, increase confidence and perhaps performance, and also strengthen social identities.

But it is far too simplistic to assume that rituals are always beneficial, or that the innocuous, repetitive quirks developed by a single individual to deal with stressful situations—such as me poring over the details of my crash, or preferring to choose the same seat every time I fly—are the same as the rigid, prescribed rituals that can be difficult and divisive.

'Rituals require a person to invest time and energy into completing actions, often without immediate instrumental value,' suggested one article.[12] In fact, the vast majority of recorded history portrays rituals of this kind, stretching all the way back to antiquity.

Consider the Metal Ages, or the three millennia BC, in Europe. One of the most interesting rituals from this time is that of hoarding. Hoarders deliberately hid or saved hundreds of objects, commonly in wet areas like bogs and rivers, or in tombs. In modern-day Romania, anthropologists have discovered thousands of hoards, containing up to 4 tonnes of bronze objects. In France, others have found sizeable collection of unused tools.[13]

Hoarding of this nature is the sort of ritual that compelled researchers like Willaim Irons to ask why humans engage in ritualistic activities when the benefit is not immediately clear.[14] Why deposit enormous wealth in areas from where it becomes irretrievable?

In findings from the Iron Age, with fewer hoards and more written explanations, we can decipher more of the intended meaning. One historian describes the most famous example of such a hoard at Hjortspring, Denmark, where 'a large wooden boat equipped for war with wooden shields, spears, and swords was destroyed and deposited in a small bog', in what was most likely a victory ceremony.[15]

This 'ritual destruction of an entire assemblage' was a new characteristic that was added to the rituals during the Iron Age.[16] It begs the question researchers have been asking about rituals even more emphatically: why do humans destroy resources, and spend time and energy on behaviour that does not immediately bear fruit?

Perhaps the most well-known example of ritualistic hoarding, made popular through the media today, is that of the Egyptian society under the pharaohs. In 2550 BC, the Great Pyramid of Giza was erected for King Khufu.[17] This pyramid is nothing if not a concrete, towering testament to the Egyptians' love of ritual. At that time, its shape symbolized a ramp to the heavens, meant to aid the king's soul to reach his final resting place among the other great leaders of the past. This was an important ritual for the Egyptians; the king's rule and mortuary rites were all in pursuance of Ma'at—a concept of universal stability personified by a goddess of the same name.

For the Egyptians, Ma'at was born at the time of the

creation of the universe, and she ensured that the flow of life was maintained. The circadian rhythm existed, the sun rose and set, the seasons changed, and life thrived because of Ma'at. The rulers entombed in these pyramids were seen as reincarnations of the god Horus. It was their job to ensure that the positive spirit of Ma'at was maintained during their rule, and it was their people's job to ensure that the pharaoh made it to the afterlife. Anything less than that threatened the very fabric of life—it could cause yawning chasms to open in the stability that Ma'at maintained, bringing darkness and destruction to the world.[18]

It is not surprising, then, that the Egyptian mortuary rites for their pharaohs were long and elaborate. The mummification of the bodies and the hoarding of thousands of objects (meant for use in the afterlife), were not just attempts to appease narcissistic rulers, but they were rituals that would determine whether Egyptian society would continue to function. As anthropologists finally made their way into the pyramids in the nineteenth and twentieth centuries, they found everything from weapons to jewellery. In Tutankhamun's tomb, shields and throwing sticks were found among three golden chariots, so massive that they had to be disassembled to be placed inside the tomb. Khufu himself had a 45-metre-long ship buried next to his great pyramid.

The journey to the afterlife was supposed to be long and full of danger, so the tombs also had multiple jars of vintage wine; baskets of fruit; bracelets, rings, pendants and scarabs, made of gold and other precious stones; and coconut oil and frankincense perfumes in alabaster bottles, all to help the ruler on his journey. If devotion was measured in riches, the Egyptian pharaohs had secured their way into their heaven.

▪

It is easy for us to see these ancient rituals from across the world and dismiss them as products of their time or laugh at their absurdity. It is also easy to recognize that an inordinate amount of wealth, time and energy was spent to pursue something that is most likely fictional. But when it comes to our own rituals, it becomes much harder to recognize frivolity or rigidity.

The truth is that rituals today—cloaked in the biases of the people who perform them—can be divisive, difficult and distracting. In the slow global trundle towards radicalism, rigid ideologies such as Salafi Islam[19] or Puritan Christianity[20] have used rituals to ascertain who follows the 'correct' version of religion. This follows from the social identity theories outlined above. If rituals are used to create identities, those identities can become exclusive and discerning. Those who do not perform these rigid rituals 'correctly' can find themselves excluded from these communities, with rituals dividing people instead of bringing them together.

Rigid adherence to rituals cannot come at the cost of everything else. I am not suggesting that people give up on religious duties, but how would the lives of the passengers of Flight 8303 be different if the ground control crew at

Karachi Airport had taken turns to pray on that Friday, instead of abandoning their posts in droves?

This rigidity that surrounds ritual worship in Pakistan did not develop in a vacuum. I have witnessed Pakistan change from a relatively open-minded society to one that is increasingly becoming regressive and dictatorial, and complex socio-economic and political triggers have underpinned it all. I would like to recount the downward spiral Pakistan has found itself in—with a deteriorating security situation, rising intolerance, and investors scared off by political volatility— because all of this has led to a more conservative society.

▪

I had a magical childhood. I grew up in Lahore, the chaotic, cosmopolitan city that lies in the heart of Punjab—Pakistan's largest province with a population of 120 million people. In the sprawling neighbourhood of Gulberg—which lies in the midst of the teeming city but retains the quiet, manicured existence of suburbia—I grew up in a middle-class household with a strict sense of discipline. I took the bus to Cathedral School and cycled to Forman Christian College. Like most children, I struggled with my allowance, but my mother insisted on instilling the value of sharing what we had and I recognized that I grew up with a degree of privilege.

Back in the 1970s and 1980s, when TV sets were still uncommon in most neighbourhoods, our household had a bulky TV with an antenna attached to the top. This was both a reflection of my father's engagement with the entertainment industry and a sign of upward social mobility. Back then, when there was only one TV channel we could access, the entire country would tune in to watch the dramas that it broadcast on its terrestrial network. In an effort to make sure that the neighbours did not feel left out, my mother would wheel this TV outside during the dusky evenings, passing its wire through a long extension cord, so that passers-by could either hang about on the lawn or lean on the low walls that surrounded our house, with their attention riveted by the glamorous stars on screen.

We also owned one of the few telephones in the neighbourhood, and I spent a significant portion of my childhood running up and down the street, conveying messages to neighbours from their relatives and friends. No message was too insignificant, no call too trivial.

My father had more direct ways of ensuring that his children grew up to be upright citizens. Once, in college, I was floored by a friend's confession that he turned on air conditioners in every room in his house during Lahore's scorching summers. We *had* air conditioners in every room, but the high price of electricity meant that I had to spend my formative years sharing a bedroom with the family, so that we could all benefit from running just one.

If my friend could run all the air conditioners in the house, I wanted to know how that was possible. In a conspiratorial whisper, my friend told me that he had made a deal with a lineman at the Water and Power Development Authority (WAPDA), then the local monopoly electricity supplier. Like most government institutions, WAPDA had the unenviable task of operating on insufficient funds within a creaking bureaucratic structure, so a few leakages here and there were not out of the ordinary. My friend had learnt how to tinker with the electricity meter outside his house to fix the bill. I was ecstatic! When I recounted this scheme to my father, certain that he would share in my enthusiasm and join me in railing against the unfairness of the skyrocketing utility bills thrust upon common people like us, he raised an eyebrow instead. 'I have a better idea,' he said with a smirk. 'Why don't you go get a gun and rob a bank? Skip these burdensome steps in between.' I have never felt such shame or revulsion for an idea I had pitched, before or since.

My father's work ethic is something I carry with me to this day. He worked tirelessly, despite being somewhat of a rebel in his own time. In fact, his rebellious nature had precipitated my paternal grandfather's migration to Pakistan in 1956. My grandfather had been well settled in Amroha, a small city in the state of Uttar Pradesh in India, and had had no desire to relocate. It was his eldest son's passion for acting that necessitated the move.

My grandfather had married three times. His first two wives had succumbed to complications during pregnancy and childbirth, and neither the women nor their children had survived. When my grandmother, his third wife, finally bore him a son, my grandfather prized his son beyond everything else he had. So, when his eldest, precious boy began to show an inclination for the performing arts, he was aghast. He was a member of what he considered an admirable profession: law. But back then in India, his family regularly rubbed shoulders with the likes of his father's cousin, Kamal Amrohi—a director and screenwriter known for hit movies like *Pakeezah*, *Mahal* and *Razia Sultan*.

Perturbed by the whole thing and bent on ensuring that my father did not follow in the footsteps of people from the film industry, my grandfather decided to relocate to Karachi in Pakistan. Perhaps he thought that a severing of these connections would bring his boy to his 'senses'. Obviously, this had no effect on dampening my father's obsession. I find it endlessly amusing that after getting a diploma in automobile engineering, my father, Munawar Saeed, became a veteran actor of the Pakistani entertainment industry—appearing on stage, TV, radio and film.

My grandmother had also come from a strong family in Pratapgarh, with vast political connections. She had cousins who were ministers and parliamentarians, including celebrated communist leaders and philanthropists. After relocating, she struggled immensely to adapt to a life that came with fewer privileges, but worked hard to increase the family fortunes and the fortunes of the women around her. For years, she ran a training school, teaching women how to sew and embroider.

Both of them worked tirelessly to build the house they retired in, and my father continued this tradition. His marriage to my mother—the daughter of a philosopher of international fame and a national newspaper's editor—only cemented my family's outlook towards life. My mother comes from a celebrated lineage of poets, journalists and intellectuals. Mine is a family steeped in the scholarly tradition, never shying away from fiery political debates, and with a penchant for literature.

This open-mindedness was on full display any time I visited my maternal family in Karachi. My family largely followed the Shia faith, the smaller of the two mainstream sects that exist within Islam. Despite a history of being persecuted for centuries, the Shia (especially those in Pakistan) have been involved in activism and lobbying, and are deeply appreciative of the spirit of their *ulema* or religious scholars. Andreas Rieck had the right idea when he called them Pakistan's 'assertive but beleaguered minority' in the title of his book.[21]

My family was characterized by this assertiveness and spirit for debate. I was often at my maternal grandparents' house during Muharram, the first month in the Islamic calendar. This month has particular historical significance for the Shia because of the attempted systematic genocide of the Prophet's family during this month almost 1,400 years ago. For Shias, it is a month of mourning and remembrance. Most members of the sect are sticklers for the ritual mourning during this time. Since they are so engrossed in *majalis* (gatherings that are part religious lectures and part outlets for mourning), it is often also a month when academic debates about historiography, history and jurisprudence come to the forefront.

At my *nana's* (maternal grandfather) house in Garden East (near Nishtar Park) in Karachi, all his Sunni[22] friends came for breaking the fast on the 10th of Muharram. Here, then, among the scholars and friends who visited my nana, I learnt about the sense of community and tolerance that rituals could foster. It was widely known that dissenting opinions could be expressed freely in my grandfather Syed Muhammad Taqi's house.

The atmosphere was such that I even heard people argue against the fanatic apotheosizing of Imam Hussain—one of the 14 Infallibles within Shia Islam, who is recognized as a martyr of martyrs within the Shia *and* Sunni traditions alike. In refusing to bow his head to the leader who was bent on diluting the religion for his personal benefit, Imam Hussain sacrificed most of his family in a war that came to a head in Karbala, Iraq, on the 9th and 10th of Muharram. At my grandfather's house, I once heard someone making outrageous arguments during the debates on the significance of the day; such as the idea that Imam Hussain had *not*, in fact, gone to Karbala to sacrifice everything. The person further said that the Imam had every intention of winning, but when the outcome became clear, he refused to bow his head to a power-hungry megalomaniac intent on corrupting the religion.

I had never before heard such frank debate about the Imam's intentions—which plucked him so cleanly from the assembly of the idols who were beyond reproach and criticism within religious thought and made it possible to speculate about his aims and drives. This was the extent of tolerance and respect for others' opinions on thorny issues that was displayed in that household. In those majalis, I internalized the idea that rituals did not have to be exacting prescriptions of religion—they could be both freeing and comforting.

I cherish the memories I have of those evenings even today. I remember that Rais Amrohvi used to make a speech about the 10th of Muharram, which never quite fit in the literary tradition of majalis, but was rousing in its uniqueness, post the intellectual discourse led by my grandfather with the visiting friends (from across the religious divide and having varying beliefs). My grandfather's younger brother, Jaun Elia, would follow this speech with a *marsiya* (a distinctly Shia elegiac poem about Imam Hussain's martyrdom and valour) in his peculiar rebellious style.

Over the years, I have seen this candid spirit of debate degenerate into a vitriolic, violent mess in the wider country; and the more it has happened, the more I appreciate the bubble of inclusivity my family created, nurtured and fiercely protected in its drawing rooms and gatherings at the house (that visitors had fondly dubbed the Hyde Park of Karachi). I was lucky enough to grow up in a family that had conservatives and liberals of all shades, and see the measured, tactful communication they had about values they often held very dear to their hearts, without resorting to contemptuous insults. It is a skill I wish more of us had today—a skill I have seen disappear from the public repertoire as more and more incendiary politicians and military leaders play with public sentiments and biases for electioneering over the years.

I am loath to say that I have seen the country deteriorating around me, because I am still a patriot at heart. However, as I grew up, I saw these inclusive, safe spaces gradually disappear. As this spirit faded, bureaucratic structures became more rigid and politics became more fractious. This affected more than Pakistan's image—it affected business, industry and the economy at large.

▪

Pakistan's involvement in the Afghan war precipitated a series of structural changes in the government. In 1978, a Marxist state had emerged within Afghanistan, and it was characterized by bitter political infighting and conflict. The Soviets—champions of communism in a world that was still in the throes of the Cold War—decided to intervene in Afghanistan and increase their influence using military force. Immediately, the US decided to retaliate and Pakistan became a crucial ally in the war.[23]

A home-grown Islamic 'renaissance' also began in the country, pivoting the population towards more rigid and conservative interpretations of the religion. Successive governments used censorship widely and the state became unrecognizable within a decade. But the country was also at the disposal of forces larger than itself.

The formation of a network that could move funds,

weapons and tactical help to Afghanistan sprung up overnight. These connections have withstood the test of time. Even today, Pakistan's border with Afghanistan remains porous and fraught with tensions. At the time, the Afghan mujahideen received funding from the CIA (Central Intelligence Agency) and, allegedly, training from the ISI (Inter-Services Intelligence).[24] Seeking an increase in its own political influence, Saudi Arabia decided to match US funding, and its intelligence agency, General Intelligence Directorate (GID), joined the fray.[25] Unofficial aid from rich Saudi civilians and princes and religious charities made the waters murkier.

This was a dangerous game for Pakistan, which found itself in the middle of two proxy wars: one between the US and the Soviet Union, and the other between Saudi Arabia and Iran. The latter riled up local sentiments. Both Saudi Arabia and Iran made claims to 'exceptionalism', meaning that they saw themselves as unique and somewhat superior to the rest of the world. According to Dilip Hiro, author of *Cold War in the Islamic World,* for Iran these claims stem from a long and unbroken history of uninterrupted rule, and more recently a government that claims to join Islamic beliefs with a democratic set-up. For Saudi Arabia, it comes from their ruling family (Al-Saud) and the country's oil.[26] Hiro argues that both countries spend a lot of money on defence, both are repressive, and both have been fighting proxy wars for influence across the Middle East. Historically, the Sunni–Shia divide has also inflamed and sustained their differences.[27] At the time, the political independence that oil had afforded Middle Eastern countries was seen as a victory for the Muslim world. In a bid to 'copy' these Muslim nations, Pakistan also began to veer towards the rigid understanding of Islam that most Middle Eastern countries followed.[28]

All these forces combined were becoming so prominent that I could see how free speech, thought and intellectual discourse—ideals that I had so dearly valued and grown up with—were now susceptible to attacks across the country. Public education began to focus more on puritanical Islam. Madrasas, which once focused on religious discourse, began to become more militant in nature, as money poured in from Saudi Arabia and Iran. Educational systems were shamelessly used to push agendas.

This is not a critique of any one particular state or actor; these agendas were manifold and persistent. In Afghanistan, even the US had developed and used textbooks for primary school children that taught them the alphabet using 'I is for Infidel, J for Jihad, K for Kalashnikov'.[29] It was a time when the mujahideen were in demand as righteous warriors against a creeping communist regime. It is not surprising then that Urdu and social studies texts in Pakistan began to include more vile lines about Hindus and other minorities, and pushed for an uncritical appreciation of all things Islamic.

One of the most damning indictments of this education system is an empirical study conducted in 2005 by Tariq Rahman, which asked students in madrasas, Urdu-medium and English-medium schools a set of questions meant to gauge their levels of tolerance. In Rahman's study, when asked whether Christians (a minority community) should have equal rights, only 18 per cent of madrasa students said yes, while 66 per cent of Urdu-medium students and 84 per cent of English-medium students agreed to it.[30]

These statistics are staggering! They are reflective of the burgeoning intolerance that the country has witnessed over the course of just a few decades. Marie Lall claims that during this time the slow and natural formation of Pakistan's national identity was arrested, and been replaced with an accelerated, artificial process of identity formation. The promotion of religious and ethnic definitions of what it meant to be Pakistani led to an exclusion of those who were seen as the 'other'. This new textbook content, meant to unify the nation under one identity only inflamed divisions.[31]

Over the years, government after government failed to strengthen institutions and rule of law, and plodded through socio-economic agendas that were vague at best, and detrimental to long-term economic growth at worst. Hence, they also failed to break the military's hold on the country's politics.[32]

During this time, I was growing up and becoming more interested in politics by the day. My family did not agree with the violence that student factions of political parties often promoted on college campuses, so I couldn't directly participate but had to watch only from the sidelines.

Nonetheless, I took immense interest in the direction that the country was heading. This was before the internet, when information was not so readily accessible, so I had to rely on newspapers and TV.

I remember painstakingly collecting and tabulating election results as they were announced, and maintaining meticulous records. The country was caught in a downward spiral that was both fascinating and horrifying, and I wanted to make sense of the madness. This turbulent political landscape was then overshadowed by something far more sinister—the development of homespun militant organizations.

Militant networks had been used as strategic assets in Afghanistan. As local and international aid was funnelled to Afghan militant networks through Pakistan, local militant organizations also began to crop up across the country. The Sunni Tehreek,[33] Lashkar-e-Jhangvi,[34] Lashkar-e-Taiba[35] and Sipah-e-Muhammad[36] all formed in the Punjab Province in the 1990s. Pakhtun's militant groups also became stronger, and formed ties with the Punjab Province-based organizations. Targeted killings, and bomb and machine-gun attacks on imam bargahs (religious congregation halls for Shias) and mosques went up on both sides of the sectarian divide. Between 1990 and 1997, Talbot claims that there were 581 deaths and 1,600 were injured.[37]

There were a few years that brought some economic growth, and the media was significantly liberalized in the early 2000s. Pakistan once again became a crucial player in the new war on terror post 9/11. In many ways, then,

Pakistan was caught in the midst of a fiery, international conflict for decades, and repercussions on local thought, identity and tolerance were par for the course.

▪

When I was growing up, I had access to several public centres that fostered debate. Pak Tea House and Faiz Ghar in Lahore served as hubs for liberal thinkers, as well as for Left-leaning poets and writers. Over time, their popularity waned, although there has been a recent resurgence in the same.

But even as different governments came and went, introducing and dissembling different forms of censorship and political control, there were always political dissenters who spoke up against injustices. One of these was a dear childhood friend Sabeen Mahmud—a human rights activist who founded The Second Floor (T2F), a community space modelled on places like Pak Tea House, where writers and freethinkers could gather and debate. T2F was a sanctuary for radicals.

In a country that was becoming increasingly intolerant, Sabeen fiercely protected her centre for 'intellectual poverty alleviation'.[38] She invited speakers from across the political spectrum to expound their views, and refused to bow down under political pressure. When she first approached me with the idea for T2F, I was enthusiastic. The suppression of political discourse frustrated me, and I agreed to become one of T2F's inaugural board members. Over time, and with a subsequent move to southern Africa for more than two years for work, my involvement with T2F's day-to-day operations reduced.

In April 2015, when I was travelling within Lahore, I heard that Sabeen had taken it upon herself to arrange a talk with Baloch activists after their session at the Lahore University of Management Sciences, one of Pakistan's leading business and humanities schools, was unceremoniously and abruptly cancelled. She insisted on holding the talk at T2F. Baloch activists have long been censored in Pakistan, both by the media and the state, which is threatened by any hints of separatist sentiment. Despite this, Sabeen held the talk. On her way back, with her elderly mother in the car with her, she was accosted by armed men and shot twice. She died immediately.

I was devastated. I had always admired Sabeen for her bravery and candour, and for her uncompromising defence of free speech. Whether she died as a direct result of that particular talk, or for some other reason, is still unknown. A few months later, the police arrested a gang of militants who had been attacking members of another Muslim minority (Ismailis) on buses. The man who had allegedly pulled the trigger, who was also a member of this gang, was a graduate of one of the most prestigious business schools in the country—the Institute of Business Administration (IBA), my alma mater, in Karachi. I could not comprehend how someone who was supposedly well educated and enlightened could harbour such hatred for Sabeen. He had targeted Sabeen for her views on Valentine's

Day, the burqa and a religious cleric whom he revered.[39]

Earlier, in 1988, Rais Amrohvi had also been murdered. It was widely suspected that the murder was carried out at the behest of a local ethnic political party. The men who were arrested belonged to an extremist religious group, decidedly anti-Shia in their rhetoric and their violence. It was a devastating loss. My great-uncle Amrohvi was always an attentive man. As a scholar and poet, he was enlightened and liberal, and his murder shook many across Pakistan.

Since his death, I had been lucky to be largely sheltered from the violence being carried out on religious grounds. But with Sabeen's assassination, the political turmoil that was making the country more and more intolerant had caught up with me. The vicious spread of these hateful ideologies brought about repercussions for not only activists like Sabeen but these political manoeuvrings and sectarian conflicts also had a significant effect on the country's economy and industry.

▪

Pakistan's terrorism problem resulted in foreign investors pulling money out of the country. Foreign investment inflows fell from 5 per cent of GDP in FY1983 to only 0.7 per cent of GDP by FY1990. Net capital inflows fell steadily from 6 per cent of GDP in FY1994 to a negative 5.2 per cent of GDP by FY2000 due to the financial sanctions imposed after the 1999 nuclear tests.[40] Growth rates fell across different sectors, inflation soared and unemployment spiralled out of control, leading to further resentment and vulnerability to intolerant ideologies. Both civilian and military governments were unable to check the economic decline and the rising intolerance.[41]

Consequently, individual industries suffered in Pakistan, including aviation. This increasing rigidity in religious thought, fuelled by the sociopolitical landscape, explains why air traffic controllers did not find the idea of abandoning their posts to offer prayers on the last Friday of Ramadan outrageous. Over the past few decades, I had seen a shift in how people viewed rituals—instead of offering comfort, support and a room for healthy debate, rituals were now the yardstick with which people gauged each other's piety. Thus, overt and extended displays of such piety became more and more common.

Pakistan is not the only place where this has happened. Consider Mandinga Muslims in Guinea-Bissau, and their diaspora in Portugal. In Guinea-Bissau, Mandinga and Muslim identities are considered one and the same. Some Mandinga traditions have seeped into religious contexts, and these are all accepted. But as Mandinga immigrants to Portugal are beginning to see, the Muslim community at large is not always accepting of these new-fangled rituals. For instance, in Mandinga culture, Muslim children are initiated into Quranic study through the 'writing on the hand' ritual. A Quranic verse is written on the child's hand and he or she licks it off, symbolically 'ingesting' the verse and its meaning. Some Mandinga immigrants in Portugal, influenced by the more global notions of a transnational Muslim identity, are not always in favour of a ritual that clearly has its roots in tribal culture and not in puritanical Islam. Others consider it a reaffirmation of both their Muslim and Mandinga identities.[42]

Again, it may be easy for an audience of my countrymen to dismiss the ritual as harmless or absurd, or in some cases, even a corruption of the religion they know. But consider the cost of rigidity in ritual worship. Here, especially since the sectarian wars of the 1990s, different sects have been vocal and sometimes violent in their pursuance of the 'correct' version of Islam. The way to offer namaz, the five daily prayers that Muslims must offer in the course of the day, is widely discussed in madrasas and drawing rooms. All schools are required to teach Islamic Studies, and the majority Sunni interpretation of the correct form of namaz is taught in most classrooms. In many classrooms, diverging from this form of prayer is not encouraged.

But what does this exclusivity achieve? What does the prescription of a personal ritual—meant to be between you and your god—mean when it is part of a national curriculum? If the only way to score points in school tests is to rote learn and reproduce this form of prayer, what are our children learning and what are we implicitly saying about other kinds of prayers? And why are we surprised when Shia or Ismaili Muslims are beaten or dragged out of Sunni or Salafi mosques, or vice versa, when they attempt to offer prayers there?

▪

To be fair, recent scholarship on religious extremism in Indonesia attempts to consider its many dimensions (theological, ritual, social and political), and posits that extremism in one dimension (such as ritual rigidity) may not necessarily be accompanied by extremism in another dimension (such as political extremism leading to violence).[43] But we must acknowledge that ritual rigidity comes at the cost of being less open-minded, and paves the road towards bias.

I would even go so far as to say that rituals cannot be the be-all and end-all of your life. If your entire focus is on performing prescribed rituals—or worse, if you derive your value and sense of ethical superiority from your ability to perform rituals correctly—then you are being distracted from your purpose on earth. Rituals cannot consume your life or dominate your struggle towards self-improvement. Good actions are the key to a good life.

Rituals are undoubtedly important, and as we have seen, their psychological benefits have kept social scientists from dismissing them entirely as superstitious bilge. An individual's quirks or personal rituals may boost confidence or reduce anxiety, and collective rituals can help alleviate grief after a loved one's death or anchor a person's identity, but they can also be equally divisive. Actions tempered by good intentions are equally, if not more, important than thoughtless rituals.

We cannot allow ourselves to turn into people who

aimlessly meander through life, resting on the belief that our practise of prescribed rituals will elevate us in this life or in whatever comes next. Take the calm and peace that ritual worship offers you, without drawing inflexible lines in the sand. More importantly, turn intent into action and work towards your goals.

This may seem obvious to the reader, but it was something that was truly brought into sharp contrast when my plane was about to crash. During those final moments of consciousness, I did not think about the rituals I had not performed on time—I thought only of how I had lived my life. My faith carried me through that day, and the depth of this faith was not determined by rigidity with regard to rituals.

I had not been fasting despite it being the most important day in the holy month of Ramadan. And while I gained a degree of comfort and peace from the personal rituals I started following after the crash, I do not make the mistake of single-mindedly focusing on ritual worship above all else. I have witnessed the end—if only for an ephemeral, fleeting moment—and I know what will be of paramount importance to me when it comes again: my faith and my dues to the people around me.

8

BOLD STEPS

Embracing Vulnerability as a Path to Strength

It does not take much to find examples of boldness that have changed the course of history. In fact, the stories that have cemented themselves in our collective consciousness as prime examples of boldness and bravery are usually those of battles and macho displays of bravado.

Before the crash, when I thought about boldness, I thought about the Spartans—who stood against Persian forces at the Battle of Thermopylae, 10 years after the Persians first squared off with the Athenians. The Spartans are remembered to this day. The Spartan king, Leonidas, and his army of 300 men disguised themselves as a small expeditionary force, as Sparta's religious leaders had refused to give permission for battle, and fought to the last man. While the soldiers at Thermopylae lost their lives, the Greeks won the larger battles against the Persians, and that served as a way to rally these forces.[1] This story naturally lends itself to popular retellings, so there have been many. The stand taken by the Spartans—whether borne out of heroism, desperation or a profound faith in unshakeable ideals—has resonated with millions. And while I find it to be inspiring in its own way, I feel as though it is time to expand and redefine how we view boldness.

▪

Since the crash upended my life, I have come to realize that boldness does not have to mean overt acts of heroism and bravery. In fact, it may very well be the opposite: having the strength to reject traditional, outdated ideas about suffering through pain with a stiff upper lip and refusing assistance. The simple act of asking for mental help when we most need it, even if this plea challenges some toxic (but normalized) ideas of masculinity, can be bold.

For me, the willpower I needed for my recovery was not something I had cultivated entirely on my own, nor did I have access to some miraculous fount of strength that others did not. In fact, as soon as I was able to, I sought counselling for what I had gone through. I was still in my hospital bed when I first consulted a psychologist.

On a societal level, we continue to attach stigma to seeking mental help, and speaking about psychological care remains a taboo in Pakistan. In less educated circles, all kinds of medical struggles are neatly lumped into one category: the afflicted is seen as someone having been possessed by djinns[2] or whichever kind of supernatural being is in vogue locally. A study in Karachi found that many 'comprehended depression as a natural feeling of sadness rather than a mental disorder',[3] thinking that depression could be treated by talking to someone trustworthy, praying to God, rather than seeking a mental health professional. It is true that faith can work wonders, but medical illnesses like depression need medical intervention.

I wanted to address the possibility of post-traumatic stress head on. I did not want to make the 'macho' mistake of attempting to unravel my thoughts and emotions on my own, that many in my community make, merely as a form of bravado. Actions like these are essential, that is, recognizing the signs of trauma and seeking help; they are a testament to the indomitable human spirit and remind you that you are in control of your life, and that it is up to you to strengthen your mind and character, and regain your sense of self.

This is perhaps what allowed me to travel back to Lahore four months after my crash by air on the same route, with the same airline, on the same seat. As mentioned previously, some people misunderstood this and pegged it as a public relations manoeuvre on the part of the airline. I can empathize with the anger the families of the victims felt, as they had misconstrued my attempt at achieving normalcy as a validation of the airline's safety protocols.

But if managing public relations for PIA had been my only concern, I would not have turned down a seat on the board of directors for the airline a few months after my crash. The Chairman approached me very respectfully, but I did not feel that I would be able to give the airline the time it required for a complete overhaul. But most importantly, more than anything else, I was acutely aware of the fact that my acceptance of such an offer may offend and hurt the families of the victims who had perished, and create more mistrust, even if others saw this fear as unfounded. For as long as I remain alive, there will be a visceral connection between them and me, and while it may strengthen or become more tenuous with time, this connection will oblige me to take these considerations into account.

▪

Tangentially, my relationship with PIA had also been a result of me boldly pursuing the airline as a client early in my career. I had always been a firm believer in making aggressive administrative decisions. Back in the early 2000s, when I was still the resident vice president at Citibank, I was pursuing PIA as a big-ticket client for the bank. The airline had a financing mandate worth US$50 million, and I had a great relationship with PIA's fund manager. However, when the decision was made public, I realized we had lost the mandate to another bank.

My boss at Citibank had asked me to cut my losses and focus on bringing in other clients. I was told in no uncertain terms that if I continued to pursue PIA and failed, I would be fired. But I was not willing to lay down arms just then. I called my contact at PIA, but he had left the office to avoid seeing me. Undeterred, I drove around to his house and waited. Seeing my doggedness, he took me to dinner to explain what had happened.

The decision had been out of his hands. The upper management had decided to give the mandate to the other bank, and informed him of the decision. They had even shared my proposal with the other bank, so they could improve the terms before pitching to the airline. I heard him out with a sinking feeling of despair.

I returned to Citibank the following day, unable to let go of what had just happened. I had the nagging feeling that there was something more I could do to salvage the deal, even though a reversal at that stage (after a public announcement of the deal) was highly unlikely. Still, I continued to visit the PIA office to see what else could be done. On one of these visits, I found the PIA staff scrambling to deal with a crisis of their own. The Federal Board of Revenue of Pakistan had frozen the airline's accounts after they had failed to deposit the tax on ticket sales. PIA did not have the liquidity needed to make the payment, and could not access its accounts. Things came to a screeching halt. While I sat there, employees around me frantically made calls to everyone to see what could be done.

Since I had gone there to discuss the financing mandate, the manager looked to me and stated flatly, 'If you can find a way around this, we'll give it to you.' That was all I needed to hear. At six or seven that evening, I rushed back into my office and got in touch with the London branch. Aviation credit was always approved out of London and I wanted to make sure things moved quickly. I made a case for PKR 1.5 billion in bridge financing for PIA. At the time, this was over US$28 million. I needed the money to be paid through before 9 a.m. the next day, so I was hoping the approval would come through the same night. If I was successful, I would get a financing mandate of US$65 million in return. If I was not, I knew I would be summarily fired by my supervisor in Pakistan, whose patience was stretching thin.

It was an excellent deal, and the London office moved quickly. I was at work until 2 a.m., finessing the details and making sure our proposal to PIA was airtight. Once I had the approval, I brought the staff in at 8 a.m. the next day and had a pay order released. By 8.35 a.m., I was at the PIA office with the pay order and a letter stating PIA would grant its financing mandate to Citibank in exchange for the bridge financing that would enable the organization to pay its taxes and unfreeze its accounts. By 9 a.m., the letter had been signed by the PIA officials and was on the desk of the Secretary of Finance in Islamabad.

Hence, my relationship with PIA had been cemented much earlier because of the persistence I had shown in pursuing it as a client. The airline had always been a mess, but I had only touched the surface as far as the financial infrastructure was concerned, and that too years earlier. It was not until the crash that I began to understand how much improvement the operations and aviation side also needed. Once I understood this, I had no qualms about turning down the role. But it was the possibility of hurting the sentiments of the victims' families that enabled me not to accept the board seat.

▪

While I could afford to turn down non-executive roles, I did need to weed out any fear of flying before it took root. I insisted on the same seat and airline for my own sanity and recovery, and I am glad that I did it. It kept me from developing the debilitating fear that would have gripped me had I left this unaddressed. This fear was not something I could afford to develop. I could not live my life cowering before travel, or refusing to use a particular mode of transport. Getting over this was imperative for my mental health.

I recently spoke with Zubair, the other survivor. Despite having played such an active role in his own survival, or perhaps because of it, he still struggles to fly. Every time his job as an engineer requires that he travel to Lahore or further outside Karachi, he chooses to take the train or drive. I understand the choice completely.

In terms of psychological scarring, I was luckier than Zubair because I was unconscious for a significant part of the crash. However, the media coverage of the event did not help the situation. I was fortunate enough to be shielded from graphic and sensationalized news reports while I was in the hospital, but that did not stop reporters from harassing my family for news about me. One reporter even barged into

the ICU while I was admitted there and had to be removed
by security. Zubair chose to leave the government hospital
where he was seeking treatment because of the number of
reporters who wanted to interview him, bent on getting
the first scoop. During a time that was already harrowing
for the victims and their families, news reports added to
the trauma. And we had to work on recovering our mental
health while being bombarded with this macabre curiosity.

▪

Over the next couple of years, the loss of power and control
over my own mobility, coupled with the isolation of the
sickbed, meant that I began to experience the helplessness
that victims of trauma often describe. The feelings I thought
I had dealt with, through time and therapy, came bubbling
to the surface again before my major surgeries in London.
I knew that I had to seek mental health services again, and
I set up sessions to work through this new pain.

This might seem par for the course for those of you who
live in places where seeking therapy is common, but I did
not have this luxury. Additionally, I knew that my post as
president and CEO of the BOP, and my being on the board
of directors of various important public and private sector
entities, was contingent on not just *appearing* mentally fit,
but in some ways also *being* fit. I needed to make sure
that the bank did not suffer because I carried unresolved
trauma, and that my employees across the province did not
falter in their faith in me at the helm because I appeared

weak. Thus, for me, seeking therapy was one of the boldest steps I took.

This is one of the lessons I wish to impart: in the bleakest of times, and in the most impossible circumstances, sometimes you can only break out of the rut you are in by taking an uncharacteristically bold step. This does not mean that you should dive head first into making impulsive decisions, but that you should forge a clear and determined path for yourself, and stand your ground through thick and thin.

Why not risk being the target of malicious gossip if working with a psychologist helps your mental health? Why not embark on a PhD in your 40s or 50s, or suggest a systematic overhaul of a rotten system? Why play it safe when the alternative can give rise to so much change?

Zubair certainly understood this lesson better than the rest of us. Despite seeing the plane burn and fall around him, he kept moving towards an unidentifiable exit—over the wing of a plane, through the rubble of a crumbling house, on to streets filled with chaos. Why not make this constant motion—this unrelenting placement of one foot in front of the other even when all seems lost—a more pivotal part of our personalities? Most of us will hopefully never be placed in a situation as terrifying as this. But perhaps this characteristic, when fostered and consciously pursued, could help us get that job we so desperately want or reignite the passion we had extinguished.

9

COMMUNICATION

The Transformative Impact of Genuine Interaction

I was now solidly on the road to recovery. I had spent hours on self-reflection—questioning and reaffirming my core beliefs. I had engaged with the best doctors, sought psychiatric help, and pushed my body to its limit during physiotherapy sessions. As more days passed, and I continued to obsess over the details of my ordeal, I began to form more concrete ideas about how I wanted to live my life.

My appreciation for literature and art was a product of my experiences, my family's spirited support of these fields, and my dismay at the ever-shrinking circles of tolerant thought and discourse over my lifetime. However, the crash brought a new objective into sharp focus. I had witnessed and survived an entirely preventable tragedy. The mistakes—the arrogance lodged in the system like a thorn embedded in the flesh, the lack of safety measures, the administrative chaos that prevailed after the crash and left families reeling while trying to recover their loved ones' bodies—had all been avertible had better systems been in place.

▪

The whole ordeal that my fellow passengers and I went through on 22 May 2020 came partly from a catastrophic failure in communication at all levels. If the captain had heard the frantic warning in the voice of the ground control operative—who told him the plane was higher than the required descent profile at Makli—this disaster could have been avoided. If the ground control had communicated effectively with the captain, informing him of the presence of sparks after the plane first touched down and scraped the landing strip before taking off again, he may not have ascended again to the height that he did. A small part of me even believes that if the pilot had kept up a steady line of communication with the passengers, perhaps he could have given people more time to come to terms with what was happening. I do not necessarily believe this would have saved more lives, given the logistics of the crash, but I do believe it would have brought some degree of calm within the cabin at the end. It would have afforded some dignity to the passengers who were about to lose their lives, and given them a moment to make peace with their god. As someone who has experienced this fleeting feeling, I do not take it lightly. Nor can I undersell what my communication with my god before the crash meant to me to appease the more secular among you.

My faith, reinvigorated by those seminal moments, has fuelled my will and kept me going through some very dark times—the excruciating days I spent on a physiotherapist's table or under the scalpel of yet another surgeon. Despite the pain and the isolation, I felt connected to my god on a profound level, and found solace in this connection.

My communication with my parents following the crash relieved their anguish and saved them from further agony. When news of the crash had first reached them, they were devastated. Not knowing my fate was perhaps one of the worst experiences my mother had gone through. My father, stoic to the end, said that he felt that I was alive with an unflappable certainty. I am not sure where his conviction came from, much like my own, but I know that hearing my voice on the phone was a relief to both of them.

This crash also brought me closer to my staff. My letter to the BOP employees after my accident was a major breakthrough in creating a special bond with them. In it, I briefly communicated the details of the crash, including the devastating loss of lives. I also explained that I had only sustained a few injuries and that the medical staff was taking excellent care of me. I thanked them for their prayers, and told them how the incident had strengthened my resolve to work towards their welfare and the bank's progress. It was a simple letter, brief and direct, but I cannot undermine its importance. It cemented the connection between me and my employees, many of whom had already reached out by then to express their concern. I wanted to make sure they knew my state of mind, and understood that the crash would not herald a new era of negativity or gloom.

▪

Before I had even embarked on this book, I made a conscious effort to be open about my experience. I have written op-eds and allowed reporters from local and international papers to interview me. Even as I processed my thoughts, multiple Pakistani media houses as well as British and Australian papers like *The Telegraph*,[1] *The Sun*[2] and *The Sydney Morning Herald*[3] published them. I have never attempted to curtail the spread of this story. In fact, I recently saw a translation of an interview in a Venezuelan publication, *LaPatilla*.[4] In sharing it, I hoped to both process my thoughts, and to reach out to people around the world who could benefit from my story.

This communication in which we are currently engaged—with me sharing my experience and learning with you—is a form of communication that I hold dear. The relationship between a reader and a writer is an intimate one; it is one in which the writer bares his or her soul. It is also a vulnerable relationship because I am opening myself up to criticism. I have listed every thought, fear and criticism—positive or negative—in these pages. It is an act that has given me immense solace.

This is why I can never undercut the importance of good, sincere and thorough communication. As sentient beings who are so completely and utterly dependent on good communication in order to survive and thrive, to usher in technological advancements and spark revolutions, and to record history and learn from it, I deeply regret the lack of importance we assign to good communication on a societal level. It is the cornerstone, the very foundation, of our collective development, and somehow it is relegated to the realm of the non-practical pursuits—meant only for the elite or the idealistically naïve among us. I feel that it is time to take communication more seriously, both on an individual and organizational level.

■

At our core, we are social beings. We crave communication, whether direct or artful. This is a quality that anthropologists have discovered even in the earliest humans living in the most rudimentary settlements.

The island of Sulawesi in Indonesia is a cluster of several peninsulas. With strikingly clear, azure water that lets you see through to the ocean floor, some of the biggest live coral colonies, and plenty of opportunities for diving, the island makes for a perfect tourist destination. But after 2019, it became known in the scientific community for another reason.

Hidden in the Leang Bulu' Sipong 4 cave on the island's southern tip is a striking cave painting, perhaps the earliest non-abstract art made by humans. The painting portrays an anoa (a dwarf buffalo) being hunted by half-men, half-animal creatures with spears.[5] It remains a vivid red. While chunks of the paint have fallen off or eroded over time, what remains is clearly some form of thick, viscous, vibrant paint. In the Leang Tedongnge cave on the same island, another scene depicts three wild boars—two engaged in a fight, while the third watches on. Again, a dark red or purplish mineral pigment was used to draw the large bodies of the beasts.[6] The artist even took care to draw the fur, using short but confident strokes to fill the body.

The Australian archaeologists who first wrote about these paintings estimate that they are at least 44,000 years old.[7] It is a startling discovery, changing the narrative that art first originated in present-day Europe, rivalling the cave paintings of France and Andalusia. The ubiquitous nature of these finds, scattered across so many continents, tells us one thing: humans everywhere have always loved stories. These stories are what allow us to hope, to dream, to strive towards complex goals, to ease agony, and to inspire others. It is what makes us quintessentially human.

We have come a long way from the cave paintings of old. From line drawings on rock walls to the creation of scripts, from papyrus and reed brushes to printing presses and computers, our expansion of and command over the tools of communication has grown so exponentially that we may as well be an entirely different species. The earliest records of ancient societies—those that had begun to form different types of governments and empires—show how much our predecessors valued effective communication.

The most obvious example of this is ancient Rome. While we have lost instrumental works on rhetoric (the

art of persuasion), such as Marcus Fabius Quintilianus'
Institutio Oratoria, we know that rhetoric was an 'essential
form of Roman life and culture'.[8] According to Ross King's
The Bookseller of Florence, 'It occupied the central place
in the educational curriculum, and the skill of speaking
effectively was prized as much as battlefield heroics. Persuasive
oratory was central in the Senate, at funerals, and at other
state occasions, as well as in criminal trials, which were
popular events held before huge crowds in the Forum (hence
"forensic" oratory).[9]

It is not surprising, then, that those Roman philosophers
and orators are not entirely lost to history, and still
plague students of history, governance and philosophy
in classrooms. It is a shame that more recently we have
separated communication, literature and philosophy from
more 'practical' pursuits like theories of business and
economics. Had we not done so, perhaps we would have
more effective business communication and more humane
economic policies. 'Softer' skills like communication are
no longer considered as important as technical ones in
large-scale organizations, like airlines and governments,
and among people whose primary roles are not related to
communication.

This is why I wanted to reintroduce these disparate domains
of communication, literature and philosophy to students of
other pursuits, such as those from the business, economics or
STEM (Science, Technology, Engineering and Mathematics)
fields. I wanted desperately to work towards making the

disparate domains more accessible to the masses. My lineage had a lot to do with this. I had seen the remarkable ways in which the artists and even the art-adjacent members of my family had navigated difficult topics and conversations, and I had been raised to believe that art and literature centred the human experience and left an indelible mark on the world. I was solidly entrenched in the world of economics and finance, but during my own rather limited forays into the matter, I had come to believe that literature and economics are fields that are inextricably connected.

We also see evidence of this in different societies across time. In the agro-pastoral society of Vedic India (1500–600 BC), literature wove detailed discussions about economic objectives into popular discourse—such as conversations about taxes, material prosperity, bargaining, interest rates, prices, loans and subsidies to farmers. In fact, some of the most spiritual Vedic texts scoff at the sort of asceticism that encourages followers to give up the pursuit of wealth and consider worldly wealth morally desirable.[10] In some ways, these ideas can also be considered very rudimentary formulations of capitalist thought, but they are not found in books meant solely for financial advisers. They are part of mainstream Vedic literature and spirituality.

Similarly, ancient texts of the Judaic civilization and the Greek empire have exhaustive discussions about the economy. They form the foundation of what is now referred to as 'Humanistic Economics'—in which humans act less as the cold, calculating, rational actors that heterodox economic theories portray them to be, and more as creative, moral individuals striving for self-actualization.[11]

■

In many ways, then, literature (arguably the most refined form of communication in any society) forms the basis of civilization in the same way that storytelling formed the basis of the earliest human tribes. It is so inexorably tied to the identity and economy of people that American author Ray Bradbury famously proclaimed, 'You don't have to burn books to destroy a culture. Just get people to stop reading them.'

Bradbury himself wrote science fiction—a genre that is perhaps considered frivolous, and not credited enough for the effect it has had on technological advancements. But there are multiple examples of innovative technologies in science fiction novels and shows that have compelled readers to research and develop their real-life versions

Jules Verne's 1870 novel *Twenty Thousand Leagues Under the Sea* followed Captain Nemo, who took his crew underwater to places like the lost city of Atlantis and the corals of the Red Sea on a ship that could dive to the bottom of the ocean. Over 20 years later, in the 1890s, Simon Lake invented the first submarine for the US Navy. Lake had read the book as a child, and vowed to make a similar machine when he grew up.[12]

The inventor of the mobile phone has a similar story. Martin Cooper was so inspired by the 'communicator' on *Star Trek*, that he spent years researching ways to create one.[13] Today, mobile technology is a cornerstone of the global economy, and hundreds of thousands of operations would come to a grinding halt without it.

Literature has also been a powerful tool for revolution. Charles Dickens' scathing portrayal of the economic injustices of Victorian Britain in his novels like *Hard Times* and *Oliver Twist* became a springboard for reform. Dickens was perhaps perfectly placed for such analysis: he witnessed the Industrial Revolution in Britain—when the rampant mechanization of production processes and the shift from an agrarian economy to one dominated by industry forced hordes of workers to live in cramped, unhygienic conditions with little to no job security, remuneration or protection. Dickens was joined by others like Daniel Defoe and Maria Edgeworth, who helped shape public discourse. The French and Russian Revolutions had similar literary influences, in Aleksandr Pushkin's poems and Nikolai Gogol's texts.

In the same vein, Pakistani literature—steeped in the literary traditions of South Asia—became more liberal and radical over time. Fierce works of resistance were written in all the major Pakistani languages: Punjabi, Urdu, English, Pashto, Sindhi, Siraiki, Farsi and Balochi. Pre-Partition literature had focused on uniting the masses against colonial rule and encouraged them to question draconian, authoritarian rule. Post-Partition, writers began to reflect on the socio-economic turmoil of their time, and on individual liberties and rights. From Muhammad Iqbal and Faiz Ahmad Faiz to Saadat Hasan Manto and Habib Jalib, writers engaged with difficult topics, often in blatant non-compliance with the laws of their time.

Faiz has written furiously and indignantly about the wars and bloodshed. In 1965, after border skirmishes between Pakistan and India escalated into full-scale war, he wrote:

> *Jab se be-nur hui hain shamein*
> *khaak mein dhundhta phirta hun na jaane kis ja*
> *kho gai hain meri donon ankhein*
> *tum jo waqif ho batao koi pehchaan meri*
> *is tarah hai ki har ik rag mein utar aaya hai*
> *mauj-dar-mauj kisi zahr ka qatil dariya*[14]

> Since our lights were extinguished
> I have been searching for a way to see;
> my eyes are lost, God knows where.
> You who know me, tell me who I am,
> who is a friend, and who an enemy.
> A murderous river has been unleashed
> into my veins; hatred beats in it.[15]

Meanwhile, playwrights like Manto raged against hegemonic control of the state. When Ayub Khan, a military dictator, created a system of 'basic democracy' that disenfranchised a lot of people while placing power with an electoral college, Jalib wrote:

> *Aise dastoor ko, subha-e-be-nur ko,*
> *Main nahin maanta*
> *Main nahin jaanta*

This rule, this lightless dawn
I do not acknowledge!
I do not know![16]

It is obvious that both global and Pakistani literature has never shied away from discussing politics or the economy. Additionally, in reflecting dire economic situations and unjust division of resources, it has often been the trigger for large-scale economic reforms. Politics and economics are bosom buddies anyway.

I had always believed that it was a shame that this link was not more widely recognized and celebrated, and that the fields of economics and literature were so disparate in academic circles. If large-scale data and numbers provide evidence for economic theory, then a study of economic history through the literary lens can humanize that theory. It can show us how complex forces shape the lives of ordinary people.

Dry texts containing figures about the cost of corruption in the bureaucracy cannot engage an audience of laypersons in the same way Mikhail Bulgakov's 'Diaboliad' does. In this short story, a fictional clerk has to navigate increasingly terrifying and absurd levels of bureaucracy to save his job, until the lines between reality and fantasy begin to blur, and the protagonist's disgruntlement and confusion begin to seep through the pages and frustrates the readers. Hence, literature serves as a window into the economic lives of humans, providing illustrations of economic theories.

▪

It is therefore imperative that anyone interested in the betterment of society and its sociopolitical landscape should engage with literature and art. We need to erase the unnecessary, arbitrary lines we have drawn in the sand, and make our curricula more holistic and inclusive of literary traditions, even for students strictly interested in non-literary fields. Well-rounded professionals with backgrounds in the disciplines of humanities (particularly literature and art) grant new perspectives to businesses and their modus operandi, think more creatively when finding scientific solutions to existing problems, and are inspired to innovate more. They engage with difficult conversations about societal inequities, and are often at the forefront of revolutionary thought. This is evident not just from the long-standing traditions within literature but also from the diaries and recorded thoughts of various revolutionary leaders from across the world.

I hope to add my humble contribution to these discussions, and I have made an effort to engage with multiple writers and reporters seeking to explore the issue. In fact, I remain one of the few people from the Global South, and the only one outside the West, to be featured in Scott J. Miller's *Master Mentors* series, in which thought leaders and businesspersons divulge the transformative insights they have had.

I focus on art—and not just pragmatic, utilitarian communication—because I believe the former encourages empathy in ways the latter does not. And when I allow myself to think of some of my loftier goals in life, and about what I want to leave behind after having fulfilled my basic obligations to my loved ones, this is what I wish for the most. I wish to see a more empathetic world, which runs on something more than the momentum of billions of individuals chasing their personal goals. When I think of this legacy, I am reminded why my family values art and literature so highly, and why we need to bring it back in technical and administrative domains.

10

LEGACY

The Pursuit of Lasting Influence

In a dimly lit theatre on Broadway, an experimental new musical debuted in 2015, chronicling the life of Alexander Hamilton, an American revolutionary and Founding Father. *Hamilton* was a hit not just because of its unconventional subject—the orphaned immigrant who had played a seminal role in the US' independence, in drafting its constitution, and in engineering its financial system—but also because of its style of music. The musical was a deliberately manic blend of hip hop, jazz, R&B and traditional theatre music, and it took the world by storm with its ingenuity.

In one of the play's quieter moments, a young Hamilton—bursting from the seams with enthusiasm to make a name for himself and assume command of a military regiment to fight off the British—is taken aside by President George Washington and reminded of the burdens he has assumed. Washington, who had been hesitant to let Hamilton lead an army unit, and had previously encouraged him to make a difference through more intellectual pursuits, laments how Hamilton had led his men into a massacre when he was first given command. The mistake still haunts the man, and Lin-Manuel Miranda's composition leaves no room to underestimate the weight of this encumbrance:

> Let me tell you what I wish I'd known,
> When I was young and dreamed of glory!
> You have no control:
>
> Who lives
> Who dies
> Who tells your story?
> [...]
> But remember from here on in
> [...]
> History has its eyes on you.

It was a song that really resonated with me, for capturing the overwhelming desire young men have to make a difference, and for the more measured wisdom that comes with age and allows you to step back and focus on your legacy, instead of short bursts of bravado. In the entire musical, Hamilton is obsessed with leaving a mark on the world. In another song, a statesman jokingly quips about how the legacy of a general killed in battle is secure 'and all he had to do was die'. And in a final, gut-wrenching song, Hamilton's wife sings about the mark he left on the world and the orphanage she built in his name.

It is a decidedly human trait to worry about what we are leaving behind, and I have to confess that I have come to obsess about this more since the crash. It may be a hackneyed trope in literature, but coming so close to your death and surviving because of a confounding series of miracles can set you on long brooding bouts of introspection.

▪

Immediately after the crash, when I was pulled from the wreckage and was drifting between consciousness and complete oblivion, I found myself unsure of whether I was alive. It was a curious feeling. In those brief moments in which my consciousness flickered back on, I thought I had perhaps died.

But once I was certain I had survived, I embarked on the very human quest to list all my discomforts and ask for things. I told my rescuers that I thought I had broken my back or burnt it, and that I had definitely broken my arm and leg. I wanted them to be careful, and they had to reassure me even in that state. When I reached the hospital, I immediately started asking doctors and passers-by for a phone, so I could call my mother and inform her of my survival, until one doctor kindly lent me hers. I was initially unable to connect to my mother, so I ended up speaking to my father. I wanted to save my parents from the agony of waiting for answers.

But while I had quickly recovered some of my equanimity, there were moments that forced me to keep returning to the uncertainty and emotional turmoil of those moments after the crash. Moving to another hospital, seeing the teary-eyed faces of the people who had come to visit me, and the sincerity and genuine concern in their eyes, was another such moment. For a brief period, they had not been sure of my survival either, and witnessing their emotions was a humbling experience. I did not know whether I had done something good for them; maybe something that was a trivial matter to me had left a lasting impression on them. Whatever the reason, I was simply grateful for this support at the time.

Since then, I have constantly thought about what I will leave behind. How people remember me will depend largely on how I treat them, and while I am happy with the unambitious yet essential goal of having positive interactions with everyone I meet, I do want to leave behind something more concrete.

▪

Given my family's deep connection with art and literature, I have always been deeply cognizant of the fact that I wanted to introduce a critical appreciation of literature and art in circles that did not necessarily have access to either. I am not an artist myself, and my professional circles remain cemented in the realm of the practical and the pragmatic. However, as part of my legacy, I wanted to inculcate an appreciation of art and literature in the younger men and women making their way into non-literary fields.

When I first began working as president of the BOP, I knew that I wanted to steer the bank closer to sponsoring this kind of holistic education to uplift future generations, and even sponsoring those activities that are not conventionally perceived as having a bearing on the economy (and are, thus, not on the radar of commercial organizations).

The literary festivals in Mirpur, Sukkur, Faisalabad, Karachi and Lahore are just such events that bring together local and foreign journalists, writers, activists, critics and political analysts to celebrate the multifaceted literary traditions of the subcontinent. The BOP's sponsorship of these events is a great source of pride for me, and I hope to continue to expand support to such activities across the country. In a similar vein, the BOP also sponsored cash prizes for young authors, between the ages of 10 and 18, who submitted their work to the Idara-e-Taleem-o-Aagahi's Children's Literature Festival. We introduced cash transfers for young girls enrolled in public sector schools with 80 per cent attendance, and to persons with disabilities, differently-abled transgender people and elderly artists with over 25 years of experience.

I wanted to make sure that as many segments of society as possible had access to the means of creating and accessing art, and could dabble in literature. If literature is to truly capture the zeitgeist of an era, and be representative of a plethora of diverse groups, then its creators must be diverse too. This inclusivity must be nurtured and protected fiercely by those who have the resources to do so.

This was also why the BOP chose to restore a Hungarian artist's paintings of the Sikh court in Lahore from the mid-19th century. August Schoefft had arrived in Bombay in 1838 (and in Lahore in 1841) to work on commission at a time when the Sikh court was already in decline. Schoefft revealed his drawings of Maharaja Ranjit Singh and the Sikh Court to the Vienna Salon in 1855, years after he first carried notes and preliminary sketches from the subcontinent back to his home in Europe.[1] By then, the Sikh kingdom no longer existed, but the vivid detail with which he rendered the courtiers makes his paintings priceless snapshots of the pageantry of the nobles of the time.

Tangentially, I am especially amused by the lengths Schoefft went to in order to make his paintings. When painting the Sikh temple of Darbar Sahib in Amritsar, he almost lost his life to a mob of *Nihangs* (an armed Sikh warrior order), who had mistakenly assumed that the pencil Schoefft held between his lips whilst using his paintbrush was a cigar. Smoking in the temple was sacrilege, and the furious mob began to attack and pursue the artist through the temple grounds. In attempting to escape, Schoefft suffered several bruises and also lost his jacket. He ran through a crowded bazaar and into the home of a local Indian leader, and only returned to his host's house after being thoroughly disguised as a native.[2] I could not possibly let his paintings be lost to the ravages of time.

Schoefft's paintings may have been straightforward captures of his time, but the realities embedded in his art have been interpreted and reinterpreted over and over again. An artist's product is perhaps the only symbol of permanence in this transient world. The paintings have become a part of our cultural heritage and legacy, and also of his native country, and is responsible for an irrevocable connection between the two countries. Recently, the BOP's sponsorship of the restoration of Schoefft's paintings was recognized by the Hungarian government, and I was awarded one of the country's highest civilian medal (the Hungarian Order of Merit) by the Hungarian president.

The process of restoring these paintings has been a circuitous and somewhat amusing one. I had not known of Schoefft or his legacy, and left to my own devices, perhaps I would not have initiated the project. The BOP's board had committed to the project prior to my appointment as president, but the funds had not been extended and the project had never materialized.

The Hungarian embassy had been trying to follow up for a while, and various Pakistanis had been expressing discomfort at the idea. Did I know that the president of Hungary had supported the Danish cartoons depicting the Prophet Muhammad (Peace Be Upon Him), and had I heard what he had said about Muslims? To me, these concerns became inconsequential next to the simple fact that the BOP had made a commitment to the Hungarians, and could not renege on this promise in good faith. Had we done so, we would have simply confirmed the view that we were dishonest, and possibly radical to boot. Irrespective of what the Hungarian president had said or not said, we had to show them the real face of Pakistan and Islam—which is all about tolerance and space for all.

Once we embarked on the restoration, we quickly realized that it was one of the largest projects of its kind between two countries. Recognizing the project's scale and scope, the same office that had made condescending remarks regarding Muslims, decided to give Hungary's highest civilian medal to a Muslim based in Pakistan. I did not need to wax lyrical about promoting or tarnishing Pakistan's image—the simple act of cultural exchange achieved the former. It helped us crystallize our own legacy.

▪

While I continue to cling to the idea of leaving behind a legacy that brings about a pivotal shift in our critical thinking and politics, and engages young people through the arts, I also have more urgent, practical aspirations.

Around 50 per cent of Pakistan's population hovers near or below the poverty line. With a looming economic crisis and rising costs of living, I cannot focus solely on patronizing the arts. In a country with dire economic problems, organizations and individuals must share with the government the burden of providing basic needs and resources to the lower socio-economic classes.

I believe that everyone who is in close proximity to poverty, and is witness to the devastation and dehumanization it can cause, has the desire to help. But we get caught up in the tedious, mundane tasks of everyday existence; we plan and procrastinate. Since the crash, I have begun to work towards the economic betterment of people around me with a sense of urgency that did not exist before. I have partnered with the Heritage Foundation of Pakistan to provide low-cost single-room homes and toilets to 100 families in Pono Colony village in Sindh.

This is, quite obviously, a direct result of coming face to face with death. I do not need to overanalyse this need—it is enough that it propels me forward. The crash forced home the ephemeral nature of this life in a way that words and philosophizing could not. I know now that I am living on borrowed time, and that is one of the reasons why I was so drawn to the song 'Borrowed Heaven' by The Corrs, which I replayed incessantly during my recovery.

> *You gave my life and I will give it back*
> *But before I do, I'm gonna hold it tight*
> *This is my prayer*
>
> *All body, all skin, all bone, borrowed*
> *All silky, all smooth and warm, borrowed*
> *[...]*
> *Almighty, I stand alone*
> *I know I'm living in*
>
> *Borrowed, borrowed heaven*

No one can understand the frailty of the body, skin and bone like a plane crash survivor can. My body has been through the ringer. I am compelled to treat the life I have left as a 'borrowed heaven'. When you feel as though every breath is leased, and your experiences force you to constantly wonder at how fleeting life is, you inevitably develop a sense of urgency to build something good and a preoccupation with your legacy.

▪

Nowhere is this sense more urgent than in my desire to overhaul the transportation industry. In the aftermath of the crash, experts from across different fields analysed the trajectory of the flight and its wreckage. However, systemic change to improve passenger safety remained largely absent in a country that has a woeful record with domestic flights.

I wanted to make a dent in this chaotic mismanagement of some of our most critical resources, and make sure that there is a sustained effort to engage all stakeholders of the airline industry: pilots and crew, the developers of standard operating procedures, the PCAA, and the legal and policymaking circles. That is why I decided to set up the Zafar Masud Foundation to have a dedicated organization that works on passenger safety. I am hoping that the organization will improve the industry and hold it accountable long after I am gone. I also hope that we can harness our collective outrage at the failures of the past and use it instead to productively rethink the systems that are in place.

In early 2023, when I finally began to draft the constitutional documents for the organization, I realized that

I did not want to restrict myself to the aviation industry alone. I wanted to work for the safety and security of passengers using all modes of transportation, namely, air, road and railway passengers. By helping to develop safety standards and infrastructure for all three industries—in line with global industry practices and trends—and enhancing awareness on transportation safety, I intend to overhaul industries that are fast becoming decrepit and dangerous. By having a dedicated staff to research relevant laws, legal infrastructure, transport accident statistics and causes, and to recommend and implement reforms, I could push for speedier, more concentrated change.

This clarity of thought was a direct result of the crash. With age and experience, I have also developed a dogged patience. I remind myself, almost daily, that even if I cannot achieve everything that has now become so important to me, I want to be remembered as an agent of change. Whether that change is infinitesimal in the grand scheme of things (the change in perspective brought on by a positive interaction with a stranger, for instance) or something grandiose (like the overhaul of a mindset or an industry), I hold both dearly.

▪

I hope that even if the experiences I have outlined in this book do not seem remotely relevant to you, I can still encourage you to strive towards a better understanding of the legacy *you* will leave behind. What is it you hope to be remembered for, other than providing for your family and for your nearest and dearest? Which social issue infuriated you, something that was a struggle for you to watch from afar? Whether it is discrimination based on gender or religion, or child abuse, or animal rights issues, or the preservation of historical art, there is always something you can do.

A few years ago, a small neighbourhood in Lahore called Krishan Nagar managed to retain its identity after Islamist political leaders tried to change the name to 'Islampura'. Residents, who were mostly Muslim themselves, refused to let years of history be erased to 'greenwash' an entire area. They also held on to the historical architecture instead of letting it be razed by modern development. These were not 'influential' politicians or people with vast amounts of money—they simply banded together and took a stand.

Identify and speak up for whatever is important to you. You will most likely know what boils your blood, but like most of us weighed down by the trials and tribulations of routine, you may not be actively working to remedy it. Start small—build a neighbourhood watch that looks out for the children in the area; or have patient, nuanced conversations about recognizing and correcting biases with the people in your community; or protest. Find what you can do within your capacity without worrying about whether it will be 'enough'. Do not wait to be established in your career and life before you begin to think about what your legacy will be.

It is easy to be bogged down by life, and to forget about the larger picture. Sometimes, it is even a little embarrassing to make grandiose plans—our cynicism wants to protect us from seeming pretentious. But I want to encourage everyone, no matter how young and inexperienced they are, to return to the grander schemes they harboured as children, to make a conscious effort to think about what they want to leave behind, and to strive to build that legacy.

AFTERWORD

Sometimes, the most purposeful objectives, and the purest of intentions, can run up against something so senseless and despicable that you begin to re-evaluate your beliefs. After the crash, I had certainly returned to work with the highest ideals. If you have reached this part of the book, you probably recognize this all too well.

But it has not always been an easy ride. In one of the organizations I have led, a young female employee was murdered by a colleague, allegedly for refusing his marriage proposal. The incident reminded me that there are deep-seated issues surrounding women's rights and consent in our society and culture. The sudden realization that it takes time for compassionate leadership to trickle down to individual branches has come because of the tragic loss of a young, talented woman.

It was an incident that business schools and theories of compassionate leadership do not prepare you for. Immediately, my team and I knew that we wanted to counter the nasty victim-blaming rumours—that often crop up in instances of gendered violence—and we addressed our employees to make that clear. I made sure the young woman's family was taken care of, and urged employees to cooperate with the ensuing investigation. I found most employees to be equally shaken by the shooting, and cooperative with the authorities. I also began organization-wide psychometric testing, and offered therapy to employees who needed it.

I hesitate to use a tragedy that took the life of an enthusiastic and vibrant young woman as an instrument to impart a life lesson. I do not wish to trivialize the incident by treating it in such a manner. Instead, my narration of the incident merely serves to express the shock and devastation I felt at the time, and the difficulty I had in returning to the values of leadership that I espoused—after a murder so callous, so unfeeling.

But then, it is important to practise compassion, even when solitary, heinous incidents like this one threaten to make us lose our faith in humanity. I could not allow the incident to alter my perception of the people who worked for me. I certainly ramped up security measures for my employees in its wake, but I could not let that define how I treated the vast majority of my workers. That vilification of the masses, so easy a trap to fall into, would not determine my organizational culture or my understanding of humanity. It was one of the lessons from this crash that I will always hold dear: believing in the best of every individual I encounter.

I believe this is the primary quality that we need to have, and it is not always something we are born with. Empathy is an actionable, learnable skill; even children are taught to place themselves in other people's shoes (even if they find the directive slightly confusing) and to consider how others are feeling. However, the incentive structures present at most large organizations remove empathy from consideration; when stock prices or sales become the sole means of assessing an employee's or manager's usefulness to an organization, empathy plummets. This obsession with profits also means that only one stakeholder has supremacy in the grand scheme of things—the shareholder.

The shareholder's wants and needs are prioritized above customers and employees both. This arbitrary decision makes no sense for businesses in the long run. It is imperative that 'soft' skills like empathy and communication be brought back into conversations about businesses, and that companies find ways to reward managers with these skills—especially given the move towards corporate social responsibility over the past decade or so, evidenced by consumers' demands for organizations to operate ethically.

This applies to many fields; the more we develop a collective global consciousness, the more practitioners in different fields strive to appear as rational, objective beings rather than those with emotions. As science became more advanced, scientists began to remove comments about their personal wonder and awe at the phenomenon they studied, until we arrived at the clinical style of present-day medical and scientific journals.

In a book that follows the history of climate science, Sarah Dry recounts the development of this style. The earliest glaciologists, when ascending volcanic peaks and traversing mile-thick ice sheets, wrote copious notes about how they felt on seeing these marvels for the first time.[1] Over time, the language of the scientific community became devoid of these emotions. It is understandable why those engaged in scientific endeavours would see this commentary as a frivolous distraction, but I do mourn for how this change has reduced the narratives' accessibility, and robbed them of the ability to inspire wonder and awe in the layperson.

Similarly, journalists today are taught to report with painstaking neutrality. Cover all sides and refrain from editorializing. The economy of their words is supposed to lend credibility to their voices from the ground. Further, they must not intervene, whether covering wildlife species in tropical forests or political unrest in third world countries. Intervention necessitates picking a side, and it is a slippery slope that demolishes neutrality.

Over the years, however, some reporters have taken this neutrality to extremes that robs them of any kind of empathetic response. One example, taught repeatedly in law and ethics classes for journalists, is that of Kevin Carter.[2] Carter was a South African photojournalist who was part of the self-styled Bang-Bang Club, a group of reporters who placed themselves in increasingly volatile situations during the early 1990s (when apartheid was still there in South Africa). They had become so accustomed to being dropped in the middle of conflicts and wars, hastily taking pictures and leaving, that this neutrality had become second nature.

In March 1993, Carter travelled to South Sudan to report on the famine caused by a horrific civil war. He took his most famous picture there: a picture of a young Sudanese child who had fallen over from hunger, forehead plastered on the ground and skin stretched over ribs that protruded from his little body. Behind him, a vulture stands waiting for her to die. The picture sent shockwaves throughout the world, and global aid to Sudan increased. Carter won a Pulitzer Prize for his photograph. After the accolades died down and he was questioned about what had happened to the child, people realized that he had no idea. He had taken the picture, shooed away the vulture and walked away.

This reignited the debate about ethics and empathy in reporting. Saving the child would not have made Carter party to any political group in Sudan, and yet he had chosen to remain neutral and not intervene. This lack of empathy did not add any qualitative value to the photograph or the coverage of the crisis. Commentators were up in arms about how this kind of journalism appropriated the suffering of those less fortunate. Four months after receiving the Pulitzer, Carter died by suicide.[3]

This raises important questions about what constitutes good journalism. Neutrality does not have to mean lack of empathy, and lack of empathy does not necessarily make for good reporting. Perhaps examples like this should encourage us to lead our lives with more empathy, to foster a community of interest and to offer support where we can. Perhaps the guilt I felt as a survivor could have been channelled into something more productive much earlier; I could have used it as fuel to offer support and compassion to the other victims' families. In fact, this guilt has been my primary motivation for creating a more equitable world. So perhaps it is time to subvert the negative association we have with survivor's guilt. If all of us, individually, see the privileges, wealth or positions we have as proof of our survival in an uneven, unjust world, then we should all have some degree of guilt that propels us to make changes.

'No regrets' (which was the case when I was ready to go at the time of the crash and was all set to face my god) is another sentiment that has made life difficult for me. Every human is a mere mortal, we have to leave this world sooner or later, in one way or the other, but we have to keep in mind that when we are leaving this world, there shall not be any regrets whatsoever (for not doing some things at all or perhaps for doing things differently). With that perspective all your actions towards humanity and society change for the better. 'No regrets' shall be the hallmark in making decisions in our lives to be a better human being, a better person.

It is my hope that this book communicates the urgency with which we need to create an equitable world, and is a damning indictment of the pitfalls of rigidity, narrow-mindedness and failure to understand the needs of others. I believe understanding this urgency is the only way for us to leave behind something worthwhile.

NOTES

Introduction

1   Freie, John F., 'Lessons About Dying and Death from Disasters', *Death, Dying, Culture*, Lloyd Steffen and Nate Hinerman (eds.), Brill, Leiden, 2013, 51–62, https://doi.org/10.1163/9781848881730_006. Accessed on 25 September 2024.

Flight 8303

1   All data regarding the crash in this chapter are sourced from the Pakistan Civil Aviation Authority's (PCAA) initial report of the crash. At the time of writing, the preliminary report did not include the exact conversation between ground control and the pilots. However, recordings of this conversation were leaked and uploaded on YouTube (https://www.youtube.com/watch?v=uA5PF3JMHdo). We confirmed with the PCAA that the recording was accurate and used descriptions from the preliminary report to place these quotes in the appropriate sections in the crash timeline, which we reconstructed. The full investigation report has since been made public, and it confirms this narrative, as cited in note 3 below. Civil Aviation Authority, Aircraft Accident Investigation Board Pakistan, *Preliminary Investigation Report: Accident of PIA Flight PK8303 Airbus A320-214 Reg No AP-BLD Crashed Near Karachi Airport on 22-05-2020*, 19 June 2020, https://tinyurl.com/ycxcus8u. Accessed on 10 September 2024.

2   Ibid. 11.

3   Civil Aviation Authority, Aircraft Accident Investigation Board

Pakistan, *Final Investigation Report: Accident of PIA Flight PK8303 Airbus A320-214 Registration Number AP-BLD Crashed Near Jinnah International Airport Karachi on 22nd May 2020*, 20 April 2023, 22, https://tinyurl.com/4x8zjvfk. Accessed on 18 October 2024.

4 The Karachi Aerodrome Control Service is responsible for tower control in the immediate vicinity of the Karachi Airport, while Karachi Approach provides air traffic control services for aircraft further out, using radar and other systems.

5 Civil Aviation Authority, Aircraft Accident Investigation Board Pakistan, *Preliminary Investigation Report: Accident of PIA Flight PK8303 Airbus A320-214 Reg No AP-BLD Crashed Near Karachi Airport on 22-05-2020*, 19 June 2020, https://tinyurl.com/ycxcus8u. Accessed on 10 September 2024.

6 Ibid. 11.

7 'CAA Seeks Action Against "Dangerous" Structures', *The Express Tribune*, 20 June 2020, https://tinyurl.com/37e7y5c4. Accessed on 10 September 2024.

8 A nacelle is a streamlined container for aircraft parts such as engines, fuel or equipment.

9 Civil Aviation Authority, Aircraft Accident Investigation Board Pakistan, *Preliminary Investigation Report: Accident of PIA Flight PK8303 Airbus A320-214 Reg. No, AP-BLD Crashed Near Karachi Airport on 22-05-2020*, 19 June 2020, 13, https://tinyurl.com/ycxcus8u. Accessed on 10 September 2024.

Arrogance

1 'Emirates Group Announces 2020-21 Results', *Emirates Media Centre*, 15 June 2021, https://tinyurl.com/958amvbr. Accessed on 25 September 2024.

2 The details listed in this chapter are based entirely on the *AAIB Final Investigation Reports*.

3 Civil Aviation Authority, Safety Investigation Board, *Investigation Report: Air Blue Flight ABQ-202 A-321 Reg AP-BJB Pakistan Crashed on 28 July 2010 at Margalla Hills Islamabad*, 28 December 2011, 3, https://tinyurl.com/ymkh4x2c. Accessed on 25 September 2024.

4 Ibid. 24–26.

5 Civil Aviation Authority, *Final Report: Aircraft Accident Investigation*

Report M/s Jahangir Siddiqui Air Flight – 201, Beechcraft 1900C-1 Reg # AP-BJD Crashed Shortly After Take Off from JIAP, Karachi on 05th November, 2010, 2 December 2015, 1, https://tinyurl.com/v9fss3nk. Accessed on 25 September 2024.

6   Civil Aviation Authority, *Final Report: Aircraft Accident Investigation into M/s Bhoja Air Flight BHO-213, Boeing 737-236A, Reg #AP-BKC Crashed on 20th April, 2012 Near BBIAP, Islamabad*, 21 January 2015, https://tinyurl.com/43thka82. Accessed on 25 September 2024.

7   Ibid. 28–29; Hasan, Saad, 'Bhoja Air Crash: Revelations from the CAA Report', *The Express Tribune*, 23 January 2014, https://tinyurl.com/yzzkzv22. Accessed on 25 September 2024.

8   Civil Aviation Authority, *Final Report: Aircraft Accident Investigation into M/s Bhoja Air Flight BHO-213, Boeing 737-236A, Reg #AP-BKC Crashed on 20th April, 2012 Near BBIAP, Islamabad*, 21 January 2015, 17–22, https://tinyurl.com/43thka82. Accessed on 25 September 2024.

9   Civil Aviation Authority, *Final Investigation Report: Accident of PIA Flight PK-661 ATR 42-500 Aircraft Reg No. AP-BHO Near Havelian 24 NM North of BBIAP Pakistan on 07 December 2016*, 18 November 2020, 153–154, https://tinyurl.com/6s7c7eba. Accessed on 25 September 2024.

10   Khan, M. Ilyas, 'Pakistan International Airlines Goat Slaughter Mocked', *BBC News*, 19 December 2016, https://tinyurl.com/2s46pyj7. Accessed on 25 September 2024.

11   Asghar, Mohammad, 'PIA: On a Wing and a Prayer', *Dawn*, 19 December 2016, https://tinyurl.com/35utzkx2. Accessed on 25 September 2024.

12   Jalal, Ayesha, and Sugata Bose, *Modern South Asia: History, Culture, Political Economy*, 3rd ed., Routledge, New York, NY, 2011, 42.

13   Leonard, Karen, 'The "Great Firm" Theory of the Decline of the Mughal Empire', *Comparative Studies in Society and History*, Vol. 21, No. 2 1979, 151–167, https://doi.org/10.1017/S0010417500012792. Accessed on 25 September 2024.

14   Jalal, Ayesha, and Sugata Bose, *Modern South Asia: History, Culture, Political Economy*, 3rd ed., New York, NY, 2011, 43.

15   Leonard, Karen, 'The "Great Firm" Theory of the Decline of the Mughal Empire', *Comparative Studies in Society and History*, Vol. 21, No. 2, April 1979, 151–167.

16   Roos, Dave, 'How the East India Company Became the World's Most Powerful Monopoly', *HISTORY*, 23 October 2020, https://tinyurl.com/yeykktms. Accessed on 25 September 2024.

17 Mulinge, Munyae M., and Gwen N. Lesetedi, 'Interrogating Our Past: Colonialism and Corruption in Sub-Saharan Africa', *African Journal of Political Science*, Vol. 3, No. 2, 1998, 15–28, https://www.jstor.org/stable/23493651. Accessed on 25 September 2024.

18 'African Participation and Resistance to the Trade', *Lowcountry Digital History Initiative*, https://tinyurl.com/2rww6y8w. Accessed on 25 September 2024.

19 Rodney, Walter, *How Europe Underdeveloped Africa*, Verso, London, 2018, 105.

20 'Pakistani Pilots Grounded Over "Fake Licences"', *BBC*, 25 June 2020, https://tinyurl.com/4f7588vx. Accessed on 25 September 2024.

21 'PIA Pilot License Irregularities Represent "Serious Lapse" in Safety Protocols: IATA', *Geo News*, 25 June 2020, https://tinyurl.com/4buynzzu. Accessed on 25 September 2024.

22 Greenfield, Charlotte, Joseph Sipalan, and Liz Lee, 'PIA Plane "Impounded" in Malaysia Over $14 Million Lease Dispute', *Reuters*, 15 January 2021, https://tinyurl.com/ybp4ywcs. Accessed on 25 September 2024.

23 Rais Amrohvi's 'Qataat', translated by me.

24 Robson, David, 'Why Arrogance Is Dangerously Contagious', *BBC*, 29 September 2020, https://tinyurl.com/5tkr6dh6. Accessed on 25 September 2024.

25 Zell, Ethan, Jason E. Strickhouser, Constantine Sedikides, and Mark D. Alicke, 'The Better-Than-Average Effect in Comparative Self-Evaluation: A Comprehensive Review and Meta-Analysis', *Psychological Bulletin*, Vol. 146, No. 2, 2020, 118–149, https://doi.org/10.1037/bul0000218. Accessed on 25 September 2024.

26 Sim, Jefferson Poh Thong, and Ying-Leh Ling, 'The Relationship of Arrogance Leadership, Job Commitment, and Job Satisfaction in Higher Educational Organisations in Sarawak', *Online Journal for TVET Practitioners*, Vol. 5, No. 2, 2020, 42–56, https://tinyurl.com/5dvkt928. Accessed on 25 September 2024.

Dues

1 Nessa Cole, a nurse and palliative care worker, discusses the 'existential slap' in an interview with *The Atlantic*; Dear, Jennie, 'What It's Like to Learn You're Going to Die', *The Atlantic*, 2 November 2017, https://

tinyurl.com/3y8n9m9p. Accessed on 25 September 2024.

2   Noyes, Russell Jr., and Roy Kletti, 'The Experience of Dying from Falls', *OMEGA*, Vol. 3, No. 1, 1972, 45–52, https://doi.org/10.2190/96XL-RQE6-DDXR-DUD5. Accessed on 25 September 2024.

3   Whymper, Edward, 'Alpine Mountain Climbing', *Great Travellers, Volume 4*, VM eBooks, 2016.

4   Dlin, B.M., 'The Experience of Surviving Almost Certain Death', *Advances in Psychosomatic Medicine*, Vol. 10, 1980, 111–118, https://doi.org/10.1159/000403295. Accessed on 25 September 2024.

5   Ring, Kenneth, *Life at Death: A Scientific Investigation of the Near-Death Experience*, Coward, McCann & Geoghegan, New York, NY, 1980.

6   Sabom, Michael B., *Recollections of Death: A Medical Investigation*, Harper & Row, New York, NY, 1982.

7   Greyson, Bruce, 'Incidence and Correlates of Near-Death Experiences in a Cardiac Care Unit', *General Hospital Psychiatry*, Vol. 25, No. 4, 2003, 269–276, https://doi.org/10.1016/s0163-8343(03)00042-2. Accessed on 25 September 2024.

8   Blanke, Olaf, Nathan Faivre, and Sebastian Dieguez, 'Leaving Body and Life Behind: Out-of-Body and Near-Death Experience', *The Neurology of Consciousness*, Steven Laureys, Olivia Gosseries and Giulio Tononi (eds.), Academic Press, Cambridge, MA, 2016, 323–347, https://doi.org/10.1016/B978-0-12-800948-2.00020-0. Accessed on 25 September 2024.

9   Elias, Ric, '3 Things I Learned While My Plane Crashed', *TED Talks*, https://tinyurl.com/2dzbmhfj. Accessed on 25 September 2024.

10   Niazi, Munir, 'Hamesha Dair Kar Deta Hun', *Intikhab-e-Qalam-Munir*, Khazina-e-Ilm-o-Adab, 2002, 87. Munir Niazi has not officially been translated into English, as far as we know, although unofficial translations like this (https://alisohani.wordpress.com/2022/02/01/i-always-miss-the-train-hamesha-der-kar-deta-hun-mein/) abound on the internet.

11   Steinhilber, Brianna, 'Is Your Emotional Baggage Holding You Back?', *NBC News*, 24 July 2018, https://tinyurl.com/msx84745. Accessed on 25 September 2024.

12   Følling, Ingrid S., Marit Solbjør and Anne-S Helvik, 'Previous Experiences and Emotional Baggage as Barriers to Lifestyle Change - A Qualitative Study of Norwegian Healthy Life Centre Participants', *BMC Family Practice*, Vol. 16, 2015, 73, https://doi.org/10.1186/s12875-015-0292-z. Accessed on 25 September 2024.

Goodness

1   All quotes and descriptions by Mohammad Zubair are from an interview with the author in Karachi on 28 October 2021.

2   All quotes and descriptions by Chaudhary Waqas are from a telephonic interview with the author on 9 July 2023.

3   'Bodies Pulled from Rubble after Deadly Karachi Plane Crash Kills 107', YouTube, 22 May 2020, https://tinyurl.com/2cm682jd; 'Karachi Plane Crash Survivor Describes His Escape', YouTube, 23 May 2020, https://tinyurl.com/39uw67bc. Both accessed on 28 September 2024.

4   '#PIA #PK8303 Plane Crashed in #Karachi #Pakistan Aerial View of Crashed Site', YouTube Shorts, 22 May 2020, https://tinyurl.com/3dajbsxw. Accessed on 28 September 2024.

5   All quotes and descriptions by Rizwan are from a telephonic interview with the author on 8 July 2023.

6   All quotes and descriptions by Tahir are from a telephonic interview with the author on 8 July 2023.

7   'This Is the Rescue of Zafar Masood! President Bank of Punjab - PIA PK 8303 Plane Crash in Karachi', YouTube Shorts, 22 May 2020, https://tinyurl.com/5n7jauke. Accessed on 28 September 2024.

8   The Edhi Foundation, founded by Abdul Sattar Edhi, is one of Pakistan's largest non-profit organizations. It is run entirely on donations. It provides all kinds of relief including educational services, medical care and food aid, and runs mortuaries, orphanages and rehabilitation centres. It has a fleet of 1,800 ambulances across Pakistan.

9   Freie, John F., 'Lessons About Dying and Death from Disasters', *Death, Dying, Culture*, Lloyd Steffen and Nate Hinerman (eds.), Brill, Leiden, 2013, 51–62, https://doi.org/10.1163/9781848881730_006. Accessed on 25 September 2024.

10   'Sri Lankan Factory Manager Lynched and Set on Fire in Pakistan', *Al Jazeera*, 3 December 2021, https://tinyurl.com/4au8s2j3. Accessed on 28 December 2024.

11   Douglass, Robin, *Rousseau and Hobbes: Nature, Free Will, and the Passions*, Oxford University Press, Oxford, 2015.

12   Ibid.

13   'Mencius', *Stanford Encyclopedia of Philosophy*, https://tinyurl.com/39zvu5pe. Accessed on 28 September 2024.

14   'Xunzi', https://tinyurl.com/2fpjsmvt. Accessed on 28 September 2024.

15 Locke, John, *An Essay Concerning Human Understanding*, Penguin Classics, London, 1997.

16 Hull, David L., 'On Human Nature', *PSA: Proceedings of the Biennial Meeting of the Philosophy of Science Association*, Vol. 1986, No. 2, 1986, 3–13, https://doi.org/10.1086/psaprocbienmeetp.1986.2.192787. Accessed on 25 September 2024.

17 Golding, William, *Lord of the Flies*, Faber & Faber, Harlow, 2011, 80.

18 Presley, Nicola, '*Lord of the Flies* and the Coral Island', *William Golding*, 30 June 2017, https://tinyurl.com/yk9y3snc. Accessed on 28 September 2024.

19 Bregman, Rutger, 'The Real *Lord of the Flies*: What Happened When Six Boys were Shipwrecked for 15 Months', *The Guardian*, 9 May 2020, https://tinyurl.com/5n8bv237. Accessed on 28 September 2024.

20 Ibid.

21 Ibid.

22 Shafi, Abid, 'Looking Back at the Oct 2005 Kashmir Earthquake', *Kashmir Reader*, 14 October 2021, https://tinyurl.com/mr3y4uwr. Accessed on 28 September 2024.

23 Freie, John F., 'Lessons About Dying and Death from Disasters', *Death, Dying, Culture*, Lloyd Steffen and Nate Hinerman (eds.), Brill, Leiden, 2013, 51–62, https://doi.org/10.1163/9781848881730_006. Accessed on 25 September 2024.

24 The concept of the Overton window describes the range of ideas and policies that are considered acceptable or mainstream within a given societal, political context. It states that policymakers are generally bound to act within the acceptable spectrum of ideas; with widely accepted ideas being in the middle, and those at the extremes being considered radical or unacceptable, and thereby falling outside of the window.

25 Azagba, Sunday, and Mesbah F. Sharaf, 'Psychosocial Working Conditions and the Utilization of Health Care Services', *BMC Public Health*, Vol. 11, 2011, 642, https://doi.org/10.1186/1471-2458-11-642. Accessed on 25 September 2024.

26 At the BOP, I noticed this change when the bank introduced a programme called BOP Madadgar, in which our employees volunteered to build shelters for flood-affected communities in Rojhan city. Those who volunteered had the opportunity to practise compassion themselves, and I saw a noticeable uplift in mood and a general increase in job satisfaction among the staff.

Sincerity

1   All quotes and descriptions by Bilal are from a telephonic interview with the author on 7 July 2023.

2   Hughes, Clyde, 'Pakistan Officials Finish Identifying Victims of PK-8303 Crash', *UPI*, 1 June 2020, https://tinyurl.com/2nufyka8. Accessed on 28 September 2024.

3   'In Pictures: PIA Flight PK-8303 Crashes in Karachi's Model Colony', *DAWN*, 22 May 2020, https://tinyurl.com/477e3vv2. Accessed on 28 September 2024.

4   Large pod-like structures under the aircraft's wings that surround the mechanism of the wing flaps.

5   Azam, Oonib, 'Late Announcement of Sops for Bodies' Handover Deprives Polani Family of Burial of Loved One', *The News*, 5 June 2020, https://tinyurl.com/85mft4sm. Accessed on 28 September 2024.

6   Rahman, Rabia, 'First-Hand Account: The Continuing Nightmare of the PK-8303 Crash', *DAWN*, 22 May 2021, https://tinyurl.com/vvw7r9jv. Accessed on 28 September 2024.

7   Varden, Helga, 'Kant and Lying to the Murderer at the Door ... One More Time: Kant's Legal Philosophy and Lies to Murderers and Nazis', *Journal of Social Philosophy*, Vol. 41, No. 4, 2010, 403–421, https://doi.org/10.1111/j.1467-9833.2010.01507.x. Accessed on 25 September 2024.

8   Wagner, Kim A., *The Skull of Alum Bheg: The Life and Death of a Rebel of 1857*, Hurst & Company, London, 2017, xix.

9   Ibid. 128.

10 Biswas, Soutik, 'What a Skull in an English Pub Says About India's 1857 Mutiny', *BBC*, 5 April 2018, https://tinyurl.com/mvafecn7. Accessed on 28 September 2024.

11 Safi, Michael, 'Churchill's Policies Contributed to 1943 Bengal Famine: Study', *The Guardian*, 29 March 2019, https://tinyurl.com/mvzc8tsu. Accessed on 28 September 2024.

12 Ibid.

13 Cicero, Marcus Tullius, *On Moral Duties (De Officiis)*, Andrew P. Peabody (trans.), https://tinyurl.com/yc89nuvc. Accessed on 25 September 2024.

14 Baiasu, Sorin, and Sylvie Loriaux (eds.), *Sincerity in Politics and International Relations*, Routledge, London, 2017, https://doi.org/10.4324/9780203762257. Accessed on 25 September 2024.

Miracles

1 These lines have gained popularity in recitations, social media and other discussions, and are attributed to Javed Akhtar's body of work. This is my translation.

2 'Asclepius', *Britannica*, 18 July 2024, https://tinyurl.com/2jmthdk4. Accessed on 28 September 2024.

3 The story of Moses is told in several religious texts; in the Bible (Old Testament), it is written in the 'Book of Exodus', Chapter 14. In the Torah, the same event is described as part of the Jewish Exodus from Egypt. In the Quran, the parting of the sea is mentioned in Surah Ash-Shu'ara (26:63–67).

4 The Bible (Luke 7:11–17, The Message)

5 *Sahih al-Bukhari*, Volume 4, Book 52, Hadith 192; variations of the story were popular in Islamic Studies classrooms in Pakistan.

6 O'Malley, Joseph (trans.), *Marx's Critique of Hegel's Philosophy of Right*, 1843, Oxford University Press, London, 1970, https://tinyurl.com/y2t3jrpe. Accessed on 25 September 2024.

7 Ekman, Simo K., and Michel Debacker, 'Survivability of Occupants in Commercial Passenger Aircraft Accidents', *Safety Science*, Vol. 104, 2018, 91–98, https://doi.org/10.1016/j.ssci.2017.12.039. Accessed on 25 September 2024.

Willpower

1 Doctor Adrian Wilson's note, 1 November 2021.

2 Doctor Adrian Wilson's note, 4 November 2021.

3 American Psychological Association, 'Airplane Crash Survivors Found to be in Better Mental Health than Non-Crash Air Travelers in the Long Run, Study Finds', *Science Daily*, 24 August 1999, https://tinyurl.com/5n8d9txv. Accessed on 28 September 2024.

4 Ibid.

5 'Greco-Persian Wars', *Britannica*, 13 September 2024, https://tinyurl.com/2fv5fj7p. Accessed on 28 September 2024.

6 Kinsella, Pat, 'Pheidippides: Is the Ancient Greek Marathon Runner Remembered for the Wrong Run?', *History Extra*, 30 September 2021, https://tinyurl.com/t3ar2hcp. Accessed on 28 September 2024.

7 Byerly, Rebecca, 'The Woman Who Outruns the Men, 200 Miles at

a Time', *The New York Times*, 5 December 2018, https://tinyurl.com/
y8u4284d. Accessed on 28 September 2024.

8   Ibid.

9   Robson, James P., Jr, and Meredith Troutman-Jordan, 'A Concept
Analysis of Cognitive Reframing', *Journal of Theory Construction &
Testing*, Vol. 18, No. 2, 2014, 55–59, https://tinyurl.com/ymk2fbwa.
Accessed on 25 September 2024.

10   Polemis, John, 'Reframing Defeating Beliefs and Language', *NYU
Coaching for Leadership*, https://tinyurl.com/muyj3tdm. Accessed on
28 September 2024.

Rituals

1   Hobson, Nicholas M., Juliana Schroeder, Jane L. Risen, Dimitris
Xygalatas, and Michael Inzlicht, 'The Psychology of Rituals: An
Integrative Review and Process-Based Framework', *Personality and
Social Psychology Review*, Vol. 22, No. 3, 2018, 260–284, https://doi.
org/10.1177/1088868317734944. Accessed on 25 September 2024.

2   Poggie, John J., and Carl Gersuny, 'Risk and Ritual: An Interpretation
of Fishermen's Folklore in a New England Community', *The Journal
of American Folklore*, Vol. 85, No. 335, 1972, 66–72, https://doi.
org/10.2307/539130. Accessed on 25 September 2024.

3   Boyer, Pascal, and Pierre Liénard, 'Ingredients of "Rituals" and Their
Cognitive Underpinnings', *Philosophical Transactions of the Royal
Society B, Biological Sciences*, Vol. 375, No. 1805, 2020, https://doi.
org/10.1098/rstb.2019.0439. Accessed on 25 September 2024.

4   'Repetitive Behavior: Understanding Its Meaning, Causes, and Impact',
NeuroLaunch, 22 September 2024, https://tinyurl.com/r2u2mdd.
Accessed on 25 September 2024.

5   Cotterill, Stewart T., Ross Sanders, and Dave Collins, 'Developing
Effective Pre-performance Routines in Golf: Why Don't We Ask the
Golfer?', *Journal of Applied Sport Psychology*, Vol. 22, No. 1, 2010, 51–64,
https://psycnet.apa.org/doi/10.1080/10413200903403216. Accessed on
25 September 2024.

6   Lang, M., J. Krátký, and D. Xygalatas, 'The Role of Ritual Behaviour
in Anxiety Reduction: An Investigation of Marathi Religious Practices
in Mauritius', *Philosophical Transactions of the Royal Society B,
Biological Sciences*, Vol. 375, No. 1805, 2020, https://doi.org/10.1098/

rstb.2019.0431. Accessed on 25 September 2024.

7   Karl, Johannes Alfons, and Ronald Fischer, 'Rituals, Repetitiveness and Cognitive Load: A Competitive Test of Ritual Benefits for Stress', *Human Nature*, Vol. 29, 2018, 418–441, https://doi.org/10.1007/s12110-018-9325-3. Accessed on 25 September 2024.

8   Hermanowicz, Joseph C., and Harriet P. Morgan, 'Ritualizing the Routine: Collective Identity Affirmation', *Sociological Forum*, Vol. 14, 1999, 197–214, https://doi.org/10.1023/A:1021462511364. Accessed on 25 September 2024.

9   Saroglou, Vassilis, 'Believing, Bonding, Behaving, and Belonging: The Big Four Religious Dimensions and Cultural Variation', *Journal of Cross-Cultural Psychology*, Vol. 42, No. 8, 2011, 1320–1340, https://doi.org/10.1177/0022022111412267. Accessed on 25 September 2024.

10   Wu, Qiao, 'The Structure of Ritual and the Epistemological Approach to Ritual Study', *The Journal of Chinese Sociology*, Vol. 5, 2018, 11, https://doi.org/10.1186/s40711-018-0081-x. Accessed on 25 September 2024.

11   'Millions of Shia Muslim Pilgrims Gather in Iraq for Arbaeen', *Al Jazeera*, 25 August 2024, https://tinyurl.com/546chw92. Accessed on 30 September 2024.

12   Hobson, Nicholas M., Devin Bonk, and Michael Inzlicht, 'Rituals Decrease the Neural Response to Performance Failure', *PeerJ*, Vol. 5, 2017, https://doi.org/10.7717/peerj.3363. Accessed on 25 September 2024.

13   'History of Europe: Rituals, Religion, and Art', *Britannica*, 16 September 2024, https://tinyurl.com/3sy5ktwc. Accessed on 30 September 2024.

14   William Irons has published multiple texts discussing this dilemma. These are: 'In Our Own Self Image: The Evolution of Morality, Deception, and Religion' (published in *Skeptic*), 'Morality as an Evolved Adaptation' (published in *Investigating the Biological Foundations of Morality*) and 'Morality, Religion, and Human Evolution' (published in *Religion & Science*), https://tinyurl.com/yckaawuv. Accessed on 25 September 2024.

15   'History of Europe: Rituals, Religion, and Art', *Britannica*, 16 September 2024, https://tinyurl.com/3sy5ktwc. Accessed on 30 September 2024.

16   Ibid.

17   Dash, Mike, 'Inside the Great Pyramid', *Smithsonian Magazine*, 1 September 2011, https://tinyurl.com/2rhsjcnf. Accessed on 30 September 2024.

18   Hirst, K. Kris, 'Egyptian View of Death and Their Pyramids', *ThoughtCo.*, 14 April 2019, https://tinyurl.com/ykb8k74v. Accessed on 30 September 2024.

19   Boukhars, Anouar, '"Quietist" and "Firebrand" Salafism in Algeria', *Carnegie Endowment for International Peace*, 24 November 2015, https://tinyurl.com/2ez5jef6. Accessed on 30 September 2024.

20   Hochstetler, Laurie Anne, 'Sacred Rites: Religious Rituals and the Transformation of American Puritanism', *Online Archive of University of Virginia Scholarship*, https://doi.org/10.18130/V33M0F. Accessed on 5 November 2024.

21   Rieck, Andreas, *The Shias of Pakistan: An Assertive and Beleaguered Minority*, Oxford University Press, Oxford, 2016.

22   Sunni Islam forms the largest branch of the religion, with 80–90 per cent of Muslims identifying with this sect.

23   Hiro, Dilip, *Cold War in the Islamic World: Saudi Arabia, Iran and the Struggle for Supremacy*, Oxford University Press, Oxford, 2019.

24   Weinbaum, Marvin G., 'War and Peace in Afghanistan: The Pakistani Role', *Middle East Journal*, Vol. 45, No. 1, 1991, 71–85, https://www.jstor.org/stable/4328240. Hoodbhoy, Pervez, 'Afghanistan and the Genesis of Global Jihad', *Peace Research*, Vol. 37, No. 1, 2005, 15–30, https://www.jstor.org/stable/24469676. Both accessed on 25 September 2024.

25   Hiro, Dilip, *Cold War in the Islamic World: Saudi Arabia, Iran and the Struggle for Supremacy*, Oxford University Press, Oxford, 2019, 115–117.

26   Ibid. 2–3.

27   Ibid.

28   Ibid.

29   Gannon, Kathy, *I is for Infidel: From Holy War to Holy Terror in Afghanistan*, PublicAffairs, New York, NY, 2005. Kamenetz, Anya, 'Q&A: J Is for Jihad', *npr*, 6 December 2014, https://tinyurl.com/5xbw7fk7. Malhotra, Niko, 'Islamist Education: American-funded Textbooks in Afghanistan', *WURJ*, https://tinyurl.com/3ctvkkrh. All three accessed on 30 September 2024.

30   Rahman, Tariq, 'Denizens of Alien Worlds: A Study of Education, Inequality and Polarization in Pakistan', *Journal of Islamic Studies*, Vol. 17, No. 2, 2006, 238–243, https://doi.org/10.1093/jis/etl013. Accessed on 25 September 2024.

31   Lall, Marie, 'Educate to Hate: The Use of Education in the Creation of Antagonistic National Identities in India and Pakistan', *Compare*, Vol.

38, No. 1, 2008, 103–119, https://doi.org/10.1080/03057920701467834. Accessed on 25 September 2024.

32 Talbot, Ian, *Pakistan: A Modern History*, Oxford University Press, Karachi, 2014.

33 'Profile of Sunni Tehreek', *Centre for Strategic and Contemporary Research*, 16 September 2016, https://tinyurl.com/mvjh8xj3. Accessed on 30 September 2024.

34 'Lashkar-e-Jhangvi', *Mapping Militants Project*, 1 July 2018, https://tinyurl.com/49j5cyue. Accessed on 30 September 2024.

35 'Lashkar-e-Taiba', *Mapping Militants Project*, 1 November 2018, https://tinyurl.com/yc4v9tv8. Accessed on 30 September 2024.

36 Azam, Maryam, 'Emergence of Sectarian Indigenous Militant Groups in Pakistan and Politicization of Militant Thought', *South Asian Studies*, Vol. 34, No. 2, 2019, 505–516, https://tinyurl.com/yfyxus47. Accessed on 25 September 2024.

37 Talbot, Ian, *Pakistan: A Modern History*, Oxford University Press, Karachi, 2014, 164.

38 Hafiz, Dilara, 'Three Pakistanis: All Young, All Talented, All Women', *HuffPost*, 21 January 2011, https://tinyurl.com/5n8ysezh. Accessed on 23 October 2024. The phrase is also commonly associated with Sabeen, since she used it to describe T2F's agenda in multiple talks.

39 Khan, Faraz, 'Two Years On, Still No Justice for Sabeen Mahmud', *The Express Tribune*, 25 April 2017, https://tinyurl.com/h5n8ct6t. Accessed on 30 September 2024.

40 Handbook of Statistics on Pakistan Economy 2020, State Bank of Pakistan, https://tinyurl.com/4b23uwye. Accessed on 16 December 2024.

41 Zaidi, S. Akbar, *Issues in Pakistan's Economy: A Political Economy Perspective*, Oxford University Press, Karachi, 1998.

42 Johnson, Michelle C., '"The Proof Is on My Palm": Debating Ethnicity, Islam and Ritual in a New African Diaspora', *Journal of Religion in Africa*, Vol. 36, No. 1, 2006, 50–77, https://www.jstor.org/stable/27594363. Accessed on 25 September 2024.

43 Wibisono, Susilo, Winnifred R. Louis, and Jolanda Jetten, 'A Multidimensional Analysis of Religious Extremism', *Frontiers in Psychology*, Vol. 10, 2019, https://doi.org/10.3389/fpsyg.2019.02560. Accessed on 25 September 2024.

Bold Steps

1   'Leonidas', *History*, https://tinyurl.com/3ffh7dvb. Accessed on 30 September 2024.

2   Damani, Sara Saleem, 'Mental Illness in Pakistan: A Subject of Stigma, Ridicule, and Cultural Insensitivity', *Journal of Pioneering Medical Sciences Blogs*, 28 January 2018, https://tinyurl.com/ftzduhn7. Accessed on 25 September 2024.

3   Nisar, Maheen, Rubaab M. Mohammad, Sani Fatima, Preet R. Shaikh, and Mehroze Rehman, 'Perceptions Pertaining to Clinical Depression in Karachi, Pakistan', *Cureus*, Vol. 11, No. 7, 2019, https://doi.org/10.7759/cureus.5094. Accessed on 25 September 2024.

Communication

1   Farmer, Ben, '"Miracle" Survivor of Plane Crash Reveals How His Life Was Saved by Last-minute Seat Change', *The Telegraph*, 21 May 2022, https://tinyurl.com/559nt3tc. Accessed on 30 September 2024.

2   Singh, Ethan, '"Living on Borrowed Heaven": I Was One of Only Two Miracle Survivors of a Plane Crash That Killed 98 People – A Last-minute Decision Saved My Life', *The Sun*, 21 May 2022, https://tinyurl.com/3vmwjzwc. Accessed on 30 September 2024.

3   Farmer, Ben, 'Miracle Plane Crash Survivor Credits Seat Choice for "Bonus Life"', *The Sydney Morning Herald*, 22 May 2022, https://tinyurl.com/39yh98sc. Accessed on 30 September 2024.

4   'Momento En El Que Rescatistas Sacan Con Vida A Un Banquero Del Avión En Pakistán', *LaPatilla*, 22 May 2020, https://tinyurl.com/5c9wmf5e. Accessed on 30 September 2024.

5   'Sulawesi Art: Animal Painting Found in Cave Is 44,000 Years Old', *BBC*, 12 December 2019, https://tinyurl.com/2pesmmf9. Accessed on 30 September 2024.

6   Brumm, Adam, Adhi Agus Oktaviana, Basran Burhan, Budianto Hakim, Rustan Lebe, Jian-xin Zhao, Priyatno Hadi Sulistyarto, Marlon Ririmasse, Shinatria Adhityatama, Iwan Sumantri, and Maxime Aubert, 'Oldest Cave Art Found in Sulawesi', *Science Advances*, Vol. 7, No. 3, 2021, https://doi.org/10.1126/sciadv.abd4648. Accessed on 25 September 2024.

7   Ibid.

8   King, Ross, *The Bookseller of Florence*, Chatto & Windus, London, 2021, 23.

9   Ibid.

10   Ibid.

11   Horodecka, Anna, 'The Impact of the Human Nature Concepts on the Goal of Humanistic Economics and Religious Motivated Streams of Economics (Buddhist, Islam and Christian)', *Rivista Internazionale di Scienze Sociali*, Vol. 123, No. 4, 2015, 413–445, https://www.jstor.org/stable/26151499. Accessed on 25 September 2024.

12   'Fulbright Talks | Exploring Other Worlds: The Case for Reading Science Fiction | Areej Mehdi', YouTube, 16 August 2019, https://tinyurl.com/5vrk5sj2. Accessed on 30 September 2024.

13   Ibid.

14   Faiz, Faiz Ahmad, 'Blackout', *Nuskha Hai Wafa*, Maktaba Karavan, 403.

15   Faiz, Faiz Ahmad, 'Blackout', Naomi Lazard (trans.), *Poetry.org*, https://tinyurl.com/yud855mh. Accessed on 30 September 2024.

16   Jalib, Habib, 'Dastoor', *Kuliyat e Habib Jalib*, Khalid Sharif, 1993, 129. This is my translation.

Legacy

1   'August Schoefft the Artist', *Sikh Museum*, https://tinyurl.com/2kwj7nk7. Accessed on 30 September 2024.

2   'Schoefft at Darbar Sahib', *Sikh Museum*, https://tinyurl.com/yc8r4xur. Accessed on 30 September 2024.

Afterword

1   Dry, Sarah, *Waters of the World*, Scribe UK, London, 2019.

2   Hadzialic, Sabahudin, 'Media Ethics in Professional Journalism: The Case of Kevin Carter: Essay', *Eurasia Review*, 26 October 2019, https://tinyurl.com/bdet82r6. Accessed on 30 September 2024.

3   Ibid.